Teamster
Rebellion

Teamster Rebellion

by Farrell Dobbs

MONAD PRESS, NEW YORK, 1972

Library of Congress Catalog Card Number 78-186690
Manufactured in the United States of America

First Edition, 1972

Published by Monad Press
for the Anchor Foundation, Inc.

Distributed by
Pathfinder Press, Inc.
410 West Street
New York, N. Y. 10014

To the men and women who gave
me unshakable confidence in the
working class, the rank and file of
General Drivers Local 574

Contents

Acknowledgments

Although as the author of this work I bear sole responsibility for its contents, it is in large measure a team project. Foremost among my collaborators has been Marvel Scholl, who shared with me the experiences recorded in this story. I have drawn extensively from a diary she kept during the Teamster strikes in 1934. She has also supplied valuable information about the role of the women involved in these strikes. In more general terms Marvel has helped to recall the circumstances surrounding various events I have described. As each chapter was dictated into a tape recorder Sharon Lee Finer transcribed it. She did so accurately, speedily, and with contagious enthusiasm about the project. Harry DeBoer and Ray Rainbolt read the manuscript, chapter by chapter, to verify the account given with their recollection of events. In doing so they also supplied helpful information, including the quotations used from Harry DeBoer. Jack Maloney furnished background data about prestrike wages and conditions in the Minneapolis trucking industry, as well as the quotations from him on other matters that appear in the text. Max Geldman gave consultative aid concerning passages dealing with the unemployed. V. Raymond Dunne, Jr., helped in preparing the sketch of his father's early life. After the rest of the team had done their part, George Novack took the whole manuscript in hand to give it final editing.

Both V. R. Dunne, Sr., and Carl Skoglund, who played a large part in this story, are now dead. They left behind considerable historical material in the form of tape recordings and written memoranda upon which I have drawn. As a former official of the Teamsters Union I have considerable union material in my files, especially minutes of various meetings, copies of official correspondence, and public statements. This material has been used to refresh my recollection and to assure accuracy in factual matters. A complete file of General Drivers Local 574's official paper, *The Organizer,* has also been available for reference. Use has been made as well of the Trotskyist weekly paper, *The Militant,* for the period covered. In addition there has been occasional reference to the *Minneapolis Labor Review,* official organ of the AFL Central Labor Union, and to issues of the capitalist daily papers at the time of the 1934 strikes.

Introduction

Teamster Rebellion tells a story that is extremely relevant to an understanding of the roots of today's labor movement, although almost forty years have elapsed since the events that it relates. The Minneapolis Teamster strikes of 1934 were among the most important union struggles of the thirties. They occurred at a crucial juncture in the history of the labor movement, helping to usher in a whole new period of labor militancy. The Minneapolis strikes took place during the same year as the Toledo Auto-Lite and San Francisco Longshore strikes. Arthur M. Schlesinger, Jr., writes: "The issue in Minneapolis, San Francisco, and Toledo was labor's right to self-organization and collective bargaining. In each case, an inflexibly anti-union employer policy thrust the leadership of labor into radical hands—Trotskyites in Minneapolis, Stalinists in San Francisco, Musteites in Toledo."[1]

Workers across the country viewed the success of these drives as proof that they could win on the picket lines. These victories contributed to a growing mood of confidence among the rank and file, preparing them for the organizing drives that lay ahead. The Minneapolis, San Francisco, and Toledo strike actions were an indispensable prelude to the formation of the CIO.

In many ways, Farrell Dobbs typified the union militants who were to play a leading role in the thirties radicalization. A midwestern youth without previous political experience (in 1932 he had voted for Herbert Hoover and hoped to become a judge), he learned fast with the unfolding of the Teamster strikes. Goaded into action by the hardships of the depression, he emerged from the three hard-fought strikes as secretary-treasurer of Teamsters Local 574—a battle-tested organizer who would go on to acquire a national reputation not only among teamsters, but also throughout the labor movement.[2]

By the end of this process, Dobbs was also a revolutionary socialist, having joined the Trotskyist Communist League of America shortly after the conclusion of the February strike. The story he tells is particularly valuable because it gives us an idea of how the revolutionaries of that time related to the challenge of organizing in the labor movement.

As Schlesinger indicates, the Communist League (forerunner of the Socialist Workers Party) played an important role in leading the Teamsters in Minneapolis. But if the Trotskyists were important to the successes of the Teamsters in Minneapolis, the converse was also true. It was the Communist League's first major participation in the mass arena. Its success led to the fusion of the Communist League with the Muste group, the American Workers Party, which led the Toledo strike. From this point on, radicals would regard the Trotskyists as an increasingly significant force in the working-class movement.

Eric Sevareid, then a student at the University of Minnesota and a reporter for the Minneapolis *Star,* points admiringly to some of the factors behind the strikes' success: "In the summer of 1934 the two cities were thrown into uproar by the famous truck drivers'. strike, led by the Dunne brothers, Trotskyists, who organized the strike as none had been organized before in American labor history. They had patrol cars of their own, stopping trucks entering or leaving the city, a daily strike newspaper, loud-speaker broadcasts, a commissary, and medical and ambulance services for their wounded. When they put on a funeral procession for one of their fallen, the life of the business district came to a stop on the streets."[3]

In fact, many of the tactical innovations employed by the Minneapolis Teamsters would be used by other unions in the thirties and in subsequent strike waves. The following comments by Schlesinger indicate that this resourcefulness was fully warranted: "In 1934 Minneapolis was, in addition, a citadel of the open shop. For almost a generation, the Citizens' Alliance, an association of Minneapolis employers, had used its money, its staff, and its secret informers to hold the line against unionism. Minneapolis businessmen were not, as they put it, against collective bargaining: the only trouble, as Charles W. Pillsbury said, was that 'labor leaders have interpreted it to mean that collective bargaining can come only through belonging to a union.' Or, as the founder of the Citizens' Alliance, A. W. Strong, said, 'I can conceive of dealing with a conservative and responsible labor leader, but certainly not with any of the AF of L leaders in Minneapolis.'"[4] Dobbs's close political association with V. R. Dunne, Carl Skoglund, and other members of the Communist League further developed his ability as an organizer. Recognizing this ability, former Teamsters President James R. Hoffa—who made a close study of Dobbs's organizing techniques—states: "I wouldn't agree with Farrell Dobbs's political philosophy or his economic ideology, but that man had a vision that was enormously beneficial to the labor movement. Beyond any doubt, he was the master architect of the Teamsters' over-the-road operations."[5]

Hoffa is here referring to developments that took place after the events recorded in *Teamster Rebellion*. Dobbs headed a project in which teamsters were organized by the tens of thousands in the eleven central states. His account of these exciting events is scheduled for publication in a subsequent volume.

Dobbs left the Teamsters in 1939. He was national labor secretary of the Socialist Workers Party from 1940 to 1943; editor of *The Militant* from late 1943 through 1948; national chairman of the SWP from 1949 to early 1953; and then from 1953 to 1972 he was its national secretary.

The Minneapolis strikes were an impressive and dramatic chapter in U. S. labor history. There is a great need for authentic first-hand accounts of such episodes, by active participants in the union movement. *Teamster Rebellion* helps fill that gap.

---

1. Arthur M. Schlesinger, Jr., "The Coming of the New Deal," *The Age of Roosevelt,* v. 2 (Boston: Houghton Mifflin Co., 1959), p. 393.

2. See James R. Hoffa's autobiography for an account of Dobbs's impact on the labor movement (James R. Hoffa, *The Trials of Jimmy Hoffa,* as told to Donald I. Rogers [Chicago: Henry .Regnery Co., 1970], pp. 105-111).

3. Eric Sevareid, *Not So Wild a Dream* (New York: Alfred A. Knopf, 1946), p. 57.

4. Schlesinger, p. 386.

5. Hoffa, p. 91.

Teamster Rebellion

DRIVERS, ORGANIZE!

Because of the depression, wages of all workers have been reduced, and this has resulted in the general lowering of the standard of living.

The increase in the cost of living has resulted in further wage cuts.

WHAT MUST WE DO?
The Only Answer Is ORGANIZATION!

DO YOU KNOW?

That under Section 7-A of the N.I.R.A. workers are not only granted the right to organize, but are guaranteed the right to exercise this privilege without discrimination?

DO YOU KNOW?

That the coal drivers of Minneapolis took advantage of this privilege to organize and through our organization gained a 25% wage increase?

Monster Mass Meeting
Shubert Theatre, Sunday, April 15
at 2 P. M.

will open the big campaign to organize

<u>ALL</u> Minneapolis Drivers, Helpers, Filling Station Attendants and Platform Men

Governor Floyd B. Olson
Will Speak on "The Right to Organize"

Speakers from your union will outline a definite program of organization for your approval.

Auspices of Minneapolis General Drivers and Helpers Local Union No. 574

Leaflet calling for April 15 mass meeting to which Governor Olson sent his representative.

The Making of a Revolutionary

This story began for me on a November afternoon in 1933. I was working as a yard man for the Pittsburgh Coal Company in Minneapolis, Minnesota. Grant Dunne, a driver from another company whom I had not met before, came in for a load of fuel and the foreman assigned me to help shovel it onto his truck. As we plied the No. 10 scoops Grant talked about our need for a union. He had in mind getting into General Drivers Local 574 of the International Brotherhood of Teamsters. Although I knew little about unions at the time, his remarks fell on receptive ears. A brief sketch of the path I had traveled up to that point should help to explain why.

I was born into a working-class family on July 25, 1907, in Queen City, Missouri. The family soon moved to Minneapolis where I grew up and graduated from North High School in January 1925. During the following year I worked at various jobs, including hosiery dyer, auto mechanic's helper, and truck driver. An economic slump in 1926 made jobs scarce so I beat my way to North Dakota where I worked in the harvest fields. Returning to Minneapolis in the fall, I got a job with the Western Electric Company as an installer of telephone central office equipment.

In April 1927 Marvel Scholl and I were married, after having gone together since we were seniors in high school. The following year Western Electric transferred me to its Iowa district where I was promoted in 1930 to the position of job foreman. Then in 1931 I was sent to the company's division office in Omaha, Nebraska. There they hung the label "planning engineer" on me and set me to work estimating the la-

bor costs of telephone installation projects. The following
months brought two events that affected me deeply, one in
a faraway country and the other here at home.

At that time the Japanese were invading China and one
day the Omaha newspaper carried a shocking picture of a
Shanghai scene. Running diagonally across the picture was
a high, barbed-wire fence buttressed at the base with sand-
bags. United States troops were stationed along this line guard-
ing what was called the "international settlement," an obviously
well-to-do district. Opposite them lay what was described in
the caption as a working-class quarter. It had been reduced
to a mass of rubble by Japanese artillery, but the wealthy
district stood unscathed. As a worker I felt instinctive sympathy for my Chinese counterparts who had been attacked
so brutally. It made me feel that something was basically
wrong with a world in which such a terrible thing could happen.

The second event took place on the job. I had been assigned
to the division office primarily for supervisory training which
included sitting in on the division superintendent's conferences
with his district supervisors — not to participate but to listen
and learn. By that time the post-1929 economic depression
had become severe and a session was held to compile a list
of employees for a general layoff. Among those named was
John Staley, a worker who had been with the company a
long time and who would soon be eligible for retirement under
the company's stingy pension plan. The points were made
that his layoff would enable the company to keep a younger,
more productive worker and save some pension money later
on. Because I had worked with John and drank with him,
he was more than just a name to me. What was being done
to him filled me with revulsion. It also became clear that they
were trying to make a tool out of me through their training
and I wanted no part of it.

As we have always done when something came up that affected our joint lives, Marvel and I talked about what was
happening and came to an agreement that I should leave
the Western Electric. By that time we had two daughters, Carol
and Mary Lou, and our third daughter, Sharon Lee, was
born during the following year. Our family economic problem was not a small one, but we thought we had a solution.

My position with the company entitled me to a termination
allowance of several hundred dollars. We planned to use that

to get a small business started back in Minneapolis. Once it was under way Marvel would take over the management. I would then go to the University of Minnesota to study political science and law, hopefully to become a judge and dispense some justice. When our finances permitted, Marvel would also enter the university so that eventually we could act as a team in carrying out our new course.

Naive though our plan now appears in retrospect, one thing can be said for it. More a dream than a plan, it reflected our desire to live as constructive and humane members of society.

The die was cast in September 1932. While driving from Omaha to Minneapolis we lightheartedly made up a song about joining the great army of the unemployed. After our arrival we set out on step one, trying to make a start in a small business, but we didn't get to first base. Soon the termination allowance was used up and I couldn't get any kind of a paying job. Nothing was to be found except come-ons for salespeople at a time when buyers were at a premium. We were brought face to face with the harsh reality that the day I left Western Electric we had indeed joined the great army of the unemployed.

Left to rely upon my parents for what help they could give, we lived with them on a small piece of land just outside Minneapolis. I contributed what I could for the household by raising what turned out to be a good crop of vegetables. As the harvest came in, Marvel and my mother worked long hours over a coal-burning stove in summer heat canning much of the crop for use during the following winter. That was in 1933 and in September I got the Pittsburgh Coal job through my father who was mechanical superintendent for the company.

Once again having our own means of support, Marvel, the children, and I moved into our own quarters inside the city. At the start I worked sixty hours a week, bringing home about eighteen dollars, which had to cover rent, food, clothing, and whatever else we needed. My parents still gave us a little help when they could, and we could rely on our part of the canned vegetables, which had been shared with them.

We were just squeaking by when suddenly I was cut to forty-eight hours a week. It was a welcome physical relief since coal heavers had to work like mules, but there was also a two-dollar cut in weekly pay. Then we got another economic blow. One night when we were away from home a severe cold

wave typical of Minnesota winters suddenly struck. By the
time we got home, the cold had ruined a great part of the
canned food which was stored in a closed-in but unheated
porch. The thin flesh of mere subsistence was being scraped
down to the bare bones of outright poverty.

On top of all that, I could expect to be laid off in the spring,
like coal drivers generally, since the work was seasonally
confined to the colder months of the year. And I could be
fired at any time without recourse merely at the employer's
whim. Something had to be done to improve the situation,
and that's why I told Grant Dunne I would join the union.

It wasn't quite that simple, he explained. The Local 574
business agent, Cliff Hall, had signed a closed-shop contract
involving a small number of workers in one coal yard. In
return for the union's promise to urge all organized labor
to patronize him as a "fair" employer, the owner had agreed to
employ only Local 574 members. Fearing that the deal would
fall through if an attempt was made to organize the whole
industry, Hall had lined up a majority of the executive board
against letting other coal workers into the union.

We needed to break through this obstacle, Grant stressed,
because it was important to be in the American Federation
of Labor and Local 574 had the AFL jurisdiction in our
industry. A volunteer committee of coal workers had been
formed to fight for admission into the union. Important help
was at hand from the Local 574 president, William S. Brown,
and the vice-president, George Frosig, who favored organizing
all coal workers. Brown was arranging for the volunteer committee to meet with the union's executive board to press the
issue. Grant emphasized the need for representation from Pittsburgh Coal, which was a key yard in the industry, and asked
me to participate in the forthcoming meeting. I agreed to do
so.

Our meeting with the executive board took place a few days
later. Brown opened the session by inviting us to state our
case, which we did, emphatically. After quite a hassle, the
board reversed itself and decided to take us into the union.
A general organizing campaign was launched through open
meetings sponsored by Local 574. Before long an impressive
number of workers were recruited into the union. A representative committee was then chosen from the various yards to
draw up a list of demands for submission to the employers.
By January 1934 the demands had been prepared and rat-

ified by the union membership. They centered on union recognition, increased wages, shorter hours, premium pay for overtime, improved working conditions, and job protection through a seniority system.

When presented with these demands, the employers refused to negotiate. A meeting of all coal workers was called for the evening of a work day to discuss the union's course of action. Several officials from other AFL unions came to the meeting and ganged up with Cliff Hall to prevent the taking of a strike vote. As a result many coal workers tore up their union cards in frustration and disgust. After having tried to deny us membership in the first place, union officials had once again done damage to our cause. A way had to be found to repair the situation.

The committee that had drawn up the demands forced another general membership meeting to be called for the following Sunday when the yards would be closed. That made it possible to have more workers present. The committee worked hard to promote a big turnout, asking workers who had torn up their cards to give it another try, and when Sunday came the union hall was packed. Decisions were made to give the employers forty-eight hours to begin negotiations, to hold another meeting on the day of the deadline, and in the meantime, to set up a strike committee. The employers stood pat in their refusal to negotiate, and the industry was struck on Wednesday, February 7, 1934.

The coal business was based mainly on the delivery of fuel to heat homes and buildings. In an effort to induce their customers to stock up on fuel the employers had been peddling strike rumors ever since the unionization drive began. After a time people decided it was just a trick to sell coal and many had little on hand that February day. To top it off, the thermometer fell way below zero as the walkout started. Since people couldn't do without fuel in such weather, the union was in a good strategic position.

After the AFL officials blocked the first attempt to take a strike vote, many workers had taken a standoffish attitude toward the union. They intended to wait and see whether or not it meant business. Now that the battle had started they began to pour into the strike headquarters. It was located in the AFL center at 614 First Avenue North where Local 574 had an office and held its meetings. My own experience illustrates the situation at that point.

After the first talk with Grant Dunne I had sounded out other workers in the Pittsburgh yard about joining the union. A few responded favorably but most of them held off to see what would happen. The first morning of the strike I went to the yard, told the foreman we were walking out and got the other yard men to go with me to the company garage. There we found the Pittsburgh drivers gathered. They were wondering what to do and a short discussion brought a general decision to support the union. We marched in a body to the strike headquarters which was nearby and everybody signed up for picket duty. I'll never forget the happy welcome we got from the other strikers.

About 600 workers were available as pickets. Most of them fanned out to cover the larger coal yards and skeleton lines were maintained elsewhere. As the struggle developed, picket captains shifted the forces around according to need. Among the strikers were drivers who owned their own trucks and hauled coal on a commission basis. These vehicles were used for a shuttle service at the disposal of the picket captain. Before noon of the first day, the picket detachments had swept the scab drivers off the streets, and all but a couple of the sixty-seven yards had been closed.

It didn't take long for us to run into trouble with the police. They mobilized to eject the pickets from a big yard that had been closed down and we were harassed generally by arrests. The strikers refused to be intimidated. In defiance of the cops, two truck loads of coal were dumped in front of one yard. Other picket detachments fought a three-hour running battle along a main thoroughfare to prevent the cops from convoying a scab delivery of coal to a greenhouse owned by the county sheriff.

This battle reflected a new picketing technique developed through rank-and-file initiative during the heat of action. A number of strikers had secondhand cars, often so worn that the owners had to be backyard mechanics to keep them running. These cars gave the pickets a high degree of mobility that had several tactical advantages. Constant patrols could be maintained on the lookout for scab drivers on the streets. When trouble developed at a given yard, reinforcements could be brought in quickly. If a scab delivery under police escort got through the picket line at a yard, as in the case of the sheriff's coal, the fight to stop it could be continued as it moved along the streets toward its destination.

My first knowledge of the development came when I heard some strikers talking excitedly about cruising pickets who were sweeping through the north side of town. "A guy named Harry DeBoer is leading them," one said, "and they sure are hell on wheels." This picketing technique, known at the time as cruising picket squads, was a forerunner of the flying squads later made famous by the auto workers.

Picketing day and night with little sleep, the strikers fought hard to keep the industry tied up tight. We were spurred on by the big stake we had in the outcome of the battle and our militancy was further stimulated by a growing awareness of organized labor's inherent power. With subzero weather hanging on, people were clamoring for coal, but the employers and their minions in government could find no way to break the strike. Finally the employers indicated they were ready to negotiate a settlement. The word came indirectly on the third day of the tie-up through the Regional Labor Board which had been set up under Franklin D. Roosevelt's administration.

On February 9, the Local 574 officials called a membership meeting to report a proposal for ending the strike that would take the form of a Labor Board order. The employers had agreed to recognize the union's right to represent its members, pending the outcome of an election of bargaining representatives to be conducted by the Labor Board. If the union won the election, it was reported, the employers would then negotiate a wage settlement. Cliff Hall had lined up quite a parade of speakers for the membership meeting: a judge, an alderman, a labor lawyer, and several AFL officials. They lauded the proposed settlement as though it represented the second coming of Christ. The union had made a wonderful start in the industry, they told the strikers, even though not all the demands had been won. "You have to learn to crawl," they advised, "before you can learn to walk."

After an hour or so of such talk, Miles Dunne got the floor. He was a dynamic speaker, good at thinking on his feet. The proposed settlement was meaningful, Miles said, mainly because it showed that we had the bosses on the run. They were now maneuvering in the negotiations to cheat us out of what we had won on the picket line. Toward that end they wanted to avoid dealing directly with the union. Local 574 could surely win a collective bargaining election, he pointed out, but we were asked to go back to work without assurance of a wage increase or of action on any of the other demands. Our answer to the bosses should be that the strike would continue until they made a direct settlement with the union. I thought Miles had argued cogently and I voted accordingly. However, a majority of the strikers voted to accept the proposed settlement and we went back to work the next day.

An intensive campaign followed in preparation for the mid-February collective-bargaining election in which Local 574 won a sweeping victory. Then, as Miles Dunne had predicted, the employers refused to talk about wages or anything else, except through the Labor Board. In the end they simply filed a stipulation with the Board setting a new uniform wage scale with relatively small increases and providing for time-and-a-half after forty-eight hours. All the workers made some gain in their earnings. For example, I got a six-dollar raise to twenty-two dollars a week.

Although we could surely have done better through a direct union-employer contract, significant concessions had been won from the bosses. We now had a strong union, at least in terms of its battle-tested ranks and in the useful role played by two Local 574 officials, Bill Brown and George Frosig. An important victory had been gained despite narrow-minded incompetents like Cliff Hall in the leadership. He and his kind had made it necessary for the coal workers to fight their way into the union and then to battle for the right to go on strike, only to lose much that we had won on the picket lines through bungled negotiations. Quite a few of us had become aware that this called for some drastic changes in the union officialdom.

After the strike, Hall and his henchmen began to make snide remarks around the union hall about the Dunnes being communists. Their talk interested me, but not for the reasons they intended. I was impressed by the way Grant and Miles had handled themselves during the strike. They appeared to know what had to be done, and they had the guts to do it.

One night after a meeting, I went into a beer joint across from the union hall and saw Miles Dunne standing at the bar. I took a place next to him, and after engaging in a little small talk, I came right to the point.

"Are you a communist?" I asked.

"What the hell's it to you?" he shot back.

"I heard that you are," I told him. "If it's so, I guess that's what I want to be."

I reasoned that if I joined a communist organization, I might be able to learn some of the things they knew. A few days later Miles and Grant took me to a private meeting at the home of Carl Skoglund with whom I had developed a speaking acquaintance during the strike. There for the first time I met V. R. Dunne. At that session I finally got a start on the political education I had been seeking. The outcome was that in March 1934 I joined the revolutionary socialist party, then known as the Communist League of America, which later evolved into the present-day Socialist Workers Party. Considering that I had voted for the Republican presidential candidate, Herbert Hoover, in the 1932 elections, I had come a long way politically in a little over a year under the impact of my experiences in the social crisis of that time.

In the thirty-seven years since then, I have learned a good deal from my participation in the trade-union and revolutionary socialist movements. From that standpoint I undertake this study of Minneapolis Teamster history across the turbulent years from 1934 to 1941. The coal strike was only the opening skirmish in a growing conflict that soon developed into virtual civil war. The broader Teamster strikes that followed the coal walkout set an example for all labor and helped generate militancy in the massive struggles waged later on in basic industry by the newly formed Committee for Industrial Organization.

Although Minneapolis had none of the basic industries in which the most definitive trade-union actions of that period took place, the Teamster strikes in that city were of major significance nationally because of certain special factors. A key aspect of the local situation was, of course, common to industry as a whole, namely, radicalization of the working class under the impact of severe economic depression. The main difference lay in the presence locally of revolutionary socialist cadres who proved highly capable of fusing with the mass of rebellious workers and adding vital know-how in the struggle against the capitalist ruling class. That circumstance must be comprehended in its direct relationship to the union's history in order to grasp the full meaning of the story.

Another special factor was the peculiar development of the region. For several reasons an unusual degree of trade-union consciousness and even political class consciousness had grown up within the working class, especially among older and middle-aged layers. Regional political trends had in turn given rise to a state government that was exceptionally subject to mass pressures, making it difficult for the governor to act as an outright strikebreaker.

It follows that the full meaning of the Teamster strikes of 1934 cannot be grasped without examining more closely these special factors in the situation, beginning with the background history.

Seeds of Revolt

Minneapolis lies at the edge of a vast agricultural prairieland extending westward across the Dakotas into Montana. In the nineteenth century lush pine forests reached from north of the city to the Canadian border. After the region was seized from the Indians, capitalist economic development began around wheat and lumber. By the time the lumber barons had despoiled the virgin timber, iron ore was discovered on the Mesabi range in northern Minnesota and strip mining of the ore for eastern steel mills opened a new sphere of capital investment as the lumber trade waned.

As the hub of the economic setup, Minneapolis knew the hum of saw mills while the lumber boom lasted, and for many years it remained the flour-milling center of the country. Iron foundries sprang up to produce farm implements. Wholesale houses were established, dealing in hardware, food, clothing, and other consumer products for the region. A network of railroads fanned out from the city, as did later a complex of truck lines. Freight rates for hauling the farmers' grain to market were dictated by the railroads, and the millers decided how much would be paid for it. This exploitation by the city-based tycoons was supplemented by somewhat more subtle financial manipulations carried on through the local grain exchange and the banks. It was a capitalist bonanza allowing everybody to wax fat except the workers and small farmers.

Labor-power for agriculture, industry, transportation, and commerce came from a combination of native-born and immigrant forces. Because of the seasonal nature of many jobs the native-born component was made up in considerable mea-

sure of itinerant workers drawn from other parts of the country. They toiled in the main as harvest hands, lumberjacks,
miners, and railroad construction laborers. The Industrial
Workers of the World arose primarily as a union of such
itinerant laborers. In Minneapolis the IWW set up Local 10
in the Bridge Square district, the town's skid row. From about
1910 until World War I it was one of the largest and most
important IWW locals in the midwest. Tens of thousands of
itinerant workers cleared through it on their way to various
jobs in the region.

A high degree of class consciousness existed among IWW
members, derived from the organization's record of heroic
struggles. Some of them became "double headers," that is, they
also belonged to one or another AFL craft union. As a result,
the Minnesota labor movement in general became influenced
by their militancy and their class-struggle outlook. The movement was further influenced by railroad workers who came
to Minneapolis and found jobs on the trains and in the railway repair shops. Among them were followers of Eugene V.
Debs, the great socialist and rail-union leader, who schooled
them in fundamentals of class politics. Their strike experience
gained elsewhere in the country and their political knowledge
had an impact within the local AFL.

Parallel to the influx of native-born itinerants, waves of immigrants arrived in the region from the late nineteenth century on.
They came mainly from Norway, Sweden, Germany, Finland,
and Denmark. Lured by the prospect of homesteading land
or buying it cheaply, most came with the hope of making a
better life for themselves in this country as farmers. To make
out on the land they had to have seed, implements, and livestock. There were mortgage payments to be met. Since they
were usually cheated out of a fair price for their produce and
sometimes faced an outright crop failure, the need often arose
of finding a way to get some ready cash. This frequently
brought immigrant farmers into Minneapolis looking for work.
Many had been skilled factory workers and building-trades
mechanics in the old country and were able to find employment at their trade. Others simply did the best they could to
find jobs at common labor.

Some decided to settle down in the city where in time they
were joined by thousands of other immigrants who had been
forced off their small farms. A considerable number of them
were already socialists when they arrived in this country. They

tended to join the Socialist Party of Debs's time in which they were organized into language federations according to the country of their birth. They had also gained significant trade-union experience in the old country. Consequently, as part of the city's labor force, they became trade-union militants and socialist activists in both the AFL and the IWW. This fusion of native-born and immigrant workers in labor militancy is illustrated by the careers of V. R. Dunne and Carl Skoglund, who were to emerge as central leaders of the 1934 Teamster strikes.

Vincent Raymond Dunne was born April 17, 1889, in Kansas City, Kansas. While Ray was an infant his father, a streetcar mechanic, was injured so severely he could no longer work and the family moved to the grandparents' farm at Little Falls, Minnesota. After getting only limited formal schooling, Ray went to work at fourteen as a lumberjack in the Minnesota woods. A year later he hit the road, stopping first in the North Dakota harvest fields where he joined the IWW. From there he moved to Montana, on to Washington, down the Pacific coast, and across the Southwest. Along the way he worked as a lumberjack, harvest hand, or at whatever he could find as an itinerant laborer.

During his travels he accumulated rich experience in strikes and free-speech fights conducted by the IWW. In 1908 he was sentenced to an Arkansas chain gang on a vagrancy charge, but it didn't stick. Seeing a chance to escape one day, he took off and didn't stop until he got to Minneapolis.

There he married Jennie Holm in 1914, and two children were born to them: a son, Raymond, and a daughter, Jeannette. In the city, Ray Dunne first got a job driving for an express company. While on that job he worked alongside Ray Rainbolt upon whom he had a strong political impact. Its lasting effect was shown by the prominent part Rainbolt later played in the 1934 strikes. He always credited Dunne as the one who pointed him in the right direction on the class-struggle road.

This experience shows how a revolutionary can be building toward the future in what may appear at the time as uneventful association with one's fellow workers. Later their paths separated temporarily when Ray Dunne changed jobs to become a clerk for a firm that delivered ice to be used for refrigeration in people's homes.

By this time he had developed beyond the syndicalist outlook of the IWW, which focused one-sidedly on the general strike as the key to the transformation of society. Although still loyal to the IWW, Ray had gone ahead of it politically in his understanding of the nature of the capitalist state. He was beginning to grasp the importance of building a Marxist vanguard party and he had come to consider himself a revolutionary socialist. Such was the nature of his political views when in 1915 he first met Carl Skoglund at a Minneapolis street meeting.

Carl Skoglund was born April 7, 1884, on an ancient feudal estate in Sweden where his ancestors had been serfs. As Carl entered his teens his father died, making it necessary for him, as the oldest child, to leave school and earn a living for the family. He found a job in a pulp mill where in time he became a skilled hand. Wages were low and working conditions bad in the mill, so Carl helped to organize a union and lead a strike for its recogition by the employer.

Through these experiences in the class struggle he became politically class conscious, learned many fundamentals of Marxism from other advanced workers and joined the Social Democratic Party. Later on he was called up for service in the Swedish army. When the conscripts were kept in uniform beyond the legal period of compulsory service, he became one of the leaders of a soldiers' protest movement demanding that they be demobilized. The ruling class called it "mutiny" and added this mark against him to their record of his activities as a trade-union and political militant. Having become so thoroughly blacklisted that he could scarcely find a job, in 1911 he decided to go to the United States. His intended wife remained behind and they were never rejoined; except for a brief marriage toward the end of his life, he remained single.

Upon arriving in Minnesota, Carl spent a short period on a railroad construction gang after which he went into the woods as a lumberjack. There he suffered a serious foot injury. Since he would be laid up for an extended period, the lumber company decided to scrap him as useless. He was given perfunctory emergency treatment by the company doctor and then fired. He went to Minneapolis where he sought medical care, maintaining himself by working as a janitor and boiler tender. As the injury mended and he could get around better, he worked as a building-trades mechanic, later on moving from that to a job as a car repairman in the railway shops. Having joined the Socialist Party in 1914, Carl had become one

of the left-wing leaders of the party's Scandinavian Federation when he first met Ray Dunne a year later.

In a personal memorandum to me written long afterward, Ray spoke of their early association: "Skogie, as he was affectionately called from the earliest days by his comrades and intimate friends, was my teacher and close comrade. He was not only a skilled mechanic; he was an intellectual of considerable stature. He had a fine library of Marxist literature and in most of our spare time we were together. . . . I spent a good deal of time reading books and pamphlets in between short 'curtain lectures' from Carl. At times there would be six or eight other comrades with us in his room, or in the IWW headquarters, or in the I. O. G. T. (International Order of Good Tempers) on the north side in the sawmill district, which was the headquarters of the largest Socialist Party local in Minneapolis or St. Paul. He explained the strong and the weak sides of the IWW. Even in those days he was as much at home with Wobblies as he was in the Socialist Party. Both recognized him as a leader. But he was a party man, first and always; an internationalist, of course."

Revolutionary internationalism came in for a serious test when the United States entered World War I in 1917. The ruling class seized the occasion for an assault on the militant workers and farmers. A seven-member Commission of Safety was set up by the Minnesota legislature, armed with dictatorial powers and a million-dollar budget. It led a systematic attack on the radical movement, the trade unions, and the small farmers' organizations. A sustained propaganda campaign was set in motion to whip up war hysteria. The intent was to unleash blind, chauvinistic rage against anyone accused of being "unpatriotic." Yellow paint was splashed on the houses of German immigrants. Radicals named in the capitalist press were subjected to mob harassment, some even being tarred and feathered.

The IWW, especially, was dealt severely crippling blows through legal frameup and imprisonment of its leading figures. Despite everything, militants staunchly opposed to imperialist war stood up against the pressures, waiting and looking for a chance to fight back. Among them were Ray and Carl, whom the experience further steeled as revolutionary fighters.

On the heels of the 1918 armistice the country entered a new stage of class struggle. Several major strikes took place

in basic industry, most of which were lost. The radical movement had been shaken up by the 1917 Russian Revolution
and a split resulted in the Socialist Party of the United States.
Through this split, the left wing of the SP provided the main
forces to found the Communist Party in 1919, which became
affiliated with the Third International led by Lenin and
Trotsky.

In Minnesota the Scandinavian Federation took the lead
in opting for the CP and almost all the SP left wing in the
state followed suit. Through this process Carl became a founding member of the new party and Ray joined it in 1920. Both
of them became members of the Minneapolis central committee of the party.

For the next few years, before the Communist Party became
Stalinized, it played a generally positive role in the trade unions
and the farmers' movement. The activities of Carl and Ray
enabled them to get elected as delegates from their local unions
to the Central Labor Union (CLU), a body made up of representatives from all AFL locals in the city. Ray had gotten
a job after the war as a weighmaster in a coal yard. His
function was to assign drivers for delivery of fuel orders and
to weigh each load to see that the order was properly filled.
This position enabled him to take the initiative in helping
to organize an AFL union of office workers. That in turn
put him in line for the delegateship to the CLU.

Properly led, the central body had the capacity to further
the workers' cause through the combined strength of all trade
unionists in the city. In practice, however, the AFL officialdom frequently used it instead to impose their dictatorial control over dissident local unions. Even so, revolutionists could
work to good advantage within the body. Efforts could be
made to block unjust acts by dictatorial AFL officials and
influence could be exerted to promote the building of a left
wing throughout the local union movement.

Carl's delegateship to the CLU stemmed from his role in
the railway carmen's union, an AFL craft unit. The various
railway shopcrafts were well organized in Minneapolis, which
was a large rail center, and he had earned recognition as
a leader throughout the left wing of the shopmen's unions.
He was elected district chairman of the strike committee in
the national shopmen's strikes of 1919 and 1922. In both
struggles, the workers were defeated through company strikebreaking, aided by the government, and because of misleader-

ship in top union circles. After the 1922 strike Carl was black-listed on the railroads, as he had been in Sweden, and he turned to driving a coal truck for a living.

After World War I a witch-hunt was set in motion, high-lighted by the Palmer raids, named after the U. S. Attorney General who ramrodded the attack on the labor movement. Radicals were jailed on a wholesale scale and many noncitizens among them were deported. Carl had a narrow escape when he went as a delegate to a Communist Party underground convention in Michigan. They were meeting in a rural wooded area when word came that a government raid was in the off-ing. Carl and another delegate were assigned to bury some papers and it turned out that the "comrade" helping him was a government agent. No greenhorn by this time, Carl escaped the dragnet and laid low until things cooled off a bit. To cap the climax, the government witch-hunt had led by 1926 to a "red" purge within the AFL. Both Carl and Ray were expelled from their unions and cut off officially from all union connections.

A more harrowing experience was soon to follow, stemming from a conflict inside the Communist Party of the Soviet Union. After V. I. Lenin died in 1924, Joseph Stalin headed up a privileged bureaucracy within the Soviet Union which grew steadily. In time it succeeded in carrying out a political counter-revolution, which stripped the masses of their democratic rights in the first workers' state. The Stalinist bureaucracy also steered the parties of the Third International into reformist collab-oration with the capitalist ruling class in other countries.

Leon Trotsky organized an opposition to the Stalinist gang but it was ruthlessly crushed and its members persecuted and jailed. Trotsky himself was exiled to Alma Ata in Central Asia. But an echo of this momentous struggle was heard by some delegates at the Sixth Congress of the Communist Inter-national in 1928 even though Stalin had an unchallenged majority there.

One of the delegates to the Moscow congress from the Com-munist Party of the United States was James P. Cannon who accidentally came upon a document by Trotsky criticizing the Stalinist draft program. The document was suppressed at the congress on the pretext that Trotsky had been expelled from the Russian CP in 1927. Cannon and Maurice Spector, a leader of the Canadian CP, smuggled a copy out of Rus-sia. Then, with the help of Max Shachtman and Martin Abern,

Cannon sought to make Trotsky's views known in this country. On October 27, 1928, Cannon, Shachtman, and Abern
were expelled from the Communist Party on charges of
"Trotskyism."

Ray Dunne and Carl Skoglund had first met Jim Cannon
in 1924 when he visited Minneapolis as a national CP leader.
After that Ray became a member of the Cannon caucus in
the party. Carl had been closer to the trade unionist William
Z. Foster, also a national CP leader, than to Cannon up to
1928. When Foster backed Stalin's line, Carl joined with Ray
in supporting the Cannon group. They demanded that the
local CP officials explain why Cannon, Shachtman, and Abern
had been expelled. For this they were summarily thrown out
of the party themselves, along with some other comrades who
felt as they did. That outrageous treatment was followed by
a Stalinist campaign of slander, ostracism, and gangsterism
against them.

Ray later described their situation at that time: "Our expulsion from the CP was to both of us, Carl and me, not alone
to be sure, something like the 'cruelest cut of all'. . . . We
were, after November 1928, truly outcasts from the viewpoint
of the 'leaders' of the union movement, the Farmer-Labor
Party and the quite numerous membership of District No.
9, the third district in membership in the CP of that time. It
may be a bit difficult to believe but it would be totally wrong
to say or indicate that we were dismayed, crushed, without
confidence, or without plans for the necessary tasks that had
been so unexpectedly thrust upon us. The record I'm quite
sure bears me out, at least on that matter."

The tasks to which he referred centered on striving to support the small and poverty-stricken Trotskyist movement that
emerged from the split. As a first step toward the new movement's growth they sought to influence wavering Communist
Party members who were disturbed about the Stalinist policies. To meet their new tasks they spent a good deal of time
studying the Marxist classics and discussing how to shape
their revolutionary course. The Trotskyists organized themselves nationally as the Communist League of America (Left
Opposition). The parenthetical designation signified that they
were fighting for readmission into the CP with the normal
democratic rights of a minority to express its views during
internal discussion periods in a disciplined way, as Lenin
had taught was the correct procedure. With the passage of

time and events they hoped to win the CP back to a correct political line. The Communist League's key instrument for this effort was its weekly paper, *The Militant.* Recognizing how it could boost their political work, the Minneapolis comrades strove mightily to give the paper badly needed financial support and to build its circulation.

In 1933 the Communist League made a turn toward the building of a new revolutionary party. The German Communist Party's failure to oppose Hitler's seizure of power in Germany that year had demonstrated the political bankruptcy of the world Stalinist movement. It was clear that a revolutionary revival of the Third International was no longer possible. This imposed the task of constructing new parties throughout the world and uniting them in a new revolutionary international.

By that time, the Communist League branch in Minneapolis had grown to about forty members and close sympathizers. Among them were comrades with long and varied experience in the trade-union and radical movements. With these forces the branch was in fairly good shape to turn toward mass work as the keystone to building the new party. Objective conditions were becoming more and more favorable for that perspective as the mass radicalization of the day intensified under the pressures of economic depression. The time was ripe, Carl and Ray thought, to speed up the tempo of the Teamster campaign, which they had already been contemplating before they were thrown out of the Communist Party in 1928.

Plan of Battle

General Drivers Local 574, through which the Communist League launched its trade-union campaign, bore the stamp of business unionism. The concepts involved had been imprinted upon the American Federation of Labor by Samuel Gompers, the founding leader. When Gompers died in 1924 he was succeeded in the AFL presidency by William Green who continued the founder's policies. Business unionism was designed to win acceptance in ruling-class circles by practicing class collaboration. Toward that end AFL officials sought to conduct themselves as "labor statesmen."

Ignoring the great bulk of the nation's workers, who were left to shift for themselves as best they could, the AFL moguls focused on the organization of narrow, privileged craft unions. These were based on various strata of skilled workers. As the better paid component of the working class, their outlook could most readily be warped to the concepts of business unionism. This objective was implemented by setting up little job trusts, through closed-shop contracts with employers, under which only members of the given craft union were hired. AFL officials anxious to get ahead in the movement were taught to accredit complete sanctity to these contracts. Strict control over strikes was maintained and one craft often scabbed on another.

The AFL officialdom grew into a complacent bureaucracy enjoying high salaries and lavish expense accounts. Living in a lush world of their own, the bureaucrats took a dispassionate view of the labor movement. Oftentimes they sided with the employers against the workers. They were quick to take disciplinary action against dissidents within the unions. Distrusting and fearing the workers, they sought to regiment the rank and file on a dictatorial basis. In the process they rigged the union structure and procedures so as to perpetuate themselves in office. Thus oriented, with their faces turned firmly to the past, the AFL officials presided over a steady decline in national membership strength as the social crisis of the 1930s gathered momentum.

In 1933 Minneapolis had only a small and struggling AFL movement. It was composed of unions in construction, printing, railway shops, service trades, trucking and a few miscellaneous trades. Most of these were only skeleton organizations. Local unions in the AFL were affiliated with parent bodies set up along craft lines and usually called "International Unions." The latter term did not at all imply an internationalist working-class outlook. It simply meant that these bodies had a few local affiliates in Canada.

The parent body of the Minneapolis drivers locals was known in 1933 as the International Brotherhood of Teamsters, Chauffeurs, Stablemen, and Helpers. At the time the IBT had around 80,000 members nationally. Daniel J. Tobin had been general president of the organization since 1907 and he was a simon-pure representative of business unionism. He boasted in the *Teamsters Journal* that IBT members were "not the rubbish that have come into other organizations." The union didn't want people to join, he added, "if they are going on strike tomorrow."

Apart from teamsters and stablemen, by then more or less a thing of the past, IBT membership was confined pretty much to truck drivers, helpers, and platform workers at loading docks. Not only was the overall craft structure a narrow one, there were even narrower craft subdivisions within the organization. Members were divided up into separate local unions more or less according to the different commodities they handled. Each local union in turn zealously guarded its jurisdiction over the given subcraft on which it was based. By dividing the workers organizationally in this manner Tobin was able to run the union with an iron hand. For that purpose he also maintained a staff of general organizers who were directly responsible to him. Their primary duty was to enforce Tobin's dictates and to report any signs of dissidence within the organization. Tobin, himself, remained aloof from the rank and file. He laid down the law through the *Teamsters Journal* and called offenders onto the carpet at his headquarters in Indianapolis, Indiana.

Where the IBT had a few local unions in a city, a Teamsters Joint Council was usually formed. It was a delegated body made up of the executive board members of the various locals, which made it cozy for those involved. An official who came under membership fire in a local union could count on understanding and support from the council. As a rule an organizer was chosen from among the delegates to administer council affairs. The council had considerable leeway in supervising IBT locals within the city, provided it followed official IBT policy and carried out all specific directives from Tobin.

A Teamsters Joint Council had been formed in Minneapolis. Within it were separate locals of ice distributors, drivers handling milk routes, tea and coffee peddlers, drivers of city-owned trucks, and general drivers. There was also a taxi local whose handful of members drove individually-owned cabs. The combined membership of these locals in 1933 was less than a thousand and not a single Teamster strike had been won in the city for some twenty years.

Local 574 was chartered around 1915 as a "general" local. Although the designation meant that 574 could take in members not specifically coming under the jurisdiction of another IBT local, it was not intended to become an all-inclusive drivers' union. If enough members of a given subcraft happened to be organized into Local 574, they were to be reorganized into a local of their own. The problem had not arisen in practice, however, because Local 574 didn't prosper. It had only about seventy-five members prior to the fall of 1933. Seven officers were elected by the membership and together they constituted the local's executive board. These included the president, vice-president and a recording secretary, who kept minutes of meetings. There was also a secretary-treasurer, who was supposed to keep financial records, handle correspondence, and take care of general union affairs. Three trustees were elected to audit the financial accounts.

Except for the president, William S. Brown, who was full-time organizer for the Teamsters Joint Council, all Local 574 officers worked in the industry. Cliff Hall had, therefore, been hired as part-time business agent to handle the local's affairs. Hall, a milk driver "on loan" from his organization, took the job as a step toward realization of his personal ambition to become a union bureaucrat. The local had four or five closed-shop contracts with small companies which had been obtained in return for a promise to get union patronage for these firms. Fulfillment of the promise was undertaken by adding these firms to a "fair" list of employers posted at the AFL Central Labor Union headquarters. If difficulties developed with one of these companies, a threat was made to take it off the list, thereby implying injury to its business.

The scheme didn't work too well, as Cliff Hall explained in a letter to Tobin dated April 22, 1930. "About two weeks ago," Hall wrote, "I was called to the office of a transfer company and he told me that . . . a non-union concern went to one of his largest stops and cut the price of hauling their merchandise in approximately half, and here is the result: the first thing he does is tell me to ask the employees if they will be willing to take a $1.00 cut per week in their wages. . . . rumors are being passed about that one of the other transfer companies is going to do likewise, unless we take steps to stop the proposition. . . . On April 21. . . . a meeting was called by members of the Local for the two transfer companies who are concerned in this proposition. I might say there were quite a few remarks passed around to the extent that . . . there was only one way to organize the city of Minneapolis, that is by presenting an agreement to the concerns that are now favorable to the Union, and if these concerns do not want to sign this agreement it is the sentiment of the organization that the General Drivers #574 will consider very much going on strike."

Hall enclosed a proposed wage agreement which he asked Tobin to approve, stating that it had been "read at the local organization, three readings [as required under the IBT by-laws — FD], and passed at each one. It has also been approved by the Teamsters Joint Council No. 32."

In granting the requested approval, Tobin wrote to Hall the following day. "You, of course, understand that the approval of a wage agreement is not the endorsement of a strike, and before allowing your men to become involved in anything like a stoppage of work, it will be necessary for you to communicate with this office stating what the difference is between your local and employers, number of men that will be involved, and all other information surrounding the situation so that I, in turn, may submit same to the General Executive Board for consideration and approval. I trust |you will not have to enter into trouble of any kind and that I will hear from you that a satisfactory settlement has been reached." This exchange of letters does much to explain why the union was so impotent.

The local was also poverty-stricken financially. Its main asset was a small iron safe which one of the officers said must be guarded "because it holds our books." Two sets of books were kept, one to be shown to Tobin's traveling auditor and the other for more refined use. From time to time the local put on an organizing drive that brought in a few new members, usually temporarily. Payments of initiation fees and monthly dues in such cases were recorded informally at first. In this way the local could avoid shelling out per capita tax to Tobin on these newly recruited workers if they dropped out after a time. Tobin sometimes complained that the local didn't send in adequate membership reports so that the International could tell how much tax it had coming. His gripes didn't change the local's procedure, however, because it was a way to put a little something extra into the iron safe.

The flavor of life inside the local can best be described by recounting a story told by Bill Brown. On one occasion the secretary-treasurer, who had little formal education, was reading a financial report to a membership meeting. Whenever he came to an item listed as miscellaneous he pronounced it "missmullaneous." Finally a member, who was a bit in his cups, interrupted to demand, "Who's this damn woman you're spending all our money on?" Sputtering angrily, the secretary-treasurer threw his books into the air and stalked out of the meeting.

On balance, there was little more in Local 574 than an IBT charter with which to begin an organizing campaign. However, this in itself was of paramount importance. Workers becoming newly unionized tend to gravitate toward the official labor movement, no matter what its condition may be at the time. In Minneapolis the AFL was the dominant labor organization and Local 574 was affiliated with it. Any attempt to bypass the AFL and set up an independent union would have been self-defeating. The AFL officialdom would automatically oppose such a step by taking counter measures to draw workers into the existing union structure. Confusion and division would result from which only the bosses could benefit.

By putting a reverse twist on the "general" jurisdiction, it would be possible to derive some advantage from the nature of Local 574's charter. A successful organizing drive could flood the local with new members from all parts of the industry. Before Tobin could get around to cutting them up into subcrafts, a situation could develop that was beyond his power to control. Such potential was inherent in the trucking industry because it was strategic to the whole economic complex in a commercial city like Minneapolis. This factor made the truck drivers the most powerful body of workers in the town. Their power was further enhanced by the fact that it was difficult to use strikebreakers, since the trucks had to operate on the streets.

To get started in this promising situation two steps were necessary: first, Local 574 had to be induced to accept new members beyond its existing job-trust circle; then a drive could be launched to organize the mass of unorganized workers in the industry and open a struggle for union recognition.

The leaders of the Communist League in Minneapolis approached these tasks with a well-thought-out conception of the dynamics of the class struggle based on a study of the interrelationship between the situation's positive and negative features. Workers were radicalizing under the goad of economic depression. To mobilize them for action it was necessary to start from their existing level of understanding. In the course of battle a majority could be convinced of the correctness of the Communist League's trade-union policy. They would come to understand that misleadership within the AFL was largely responsible for the fact that not a single strike had been won by any union in the city during the previous decade. To drive the point home it was imperative to show in the opening clash with the bosses that a strike could be won.

The key to all this was the infusion of politically class-conscious leadership into the union through the cadres of the Communist League. Of course, they could not assume immediate leadership of the union. Their role as leaders would have to develop and be certified through the forthcoming struggles against the employers. To facilitate that objective it was necessary that all party members in the city understand and support the projected Teamster campaign. Toward that end the whole concept was thoroughly discussed in the party branch and firm agreement was reached on the steps to be taken. It was also necessary to decide in advance who would speak publicly for the party and lead its members in the union during the campaign.

In his memorandum mentioned previously, Ray Dunne explained how that was thought out: "Skogie proposed that I, rather than he, accept the role of party public spokesman

and leader of the party fraction. The reasons for Carl's proposal were as follows: We both knew, and he argued, that
it was a touch-and-go matter. If we were successful the employers would pick up the matter of his noncitizenship. If he
were a public spokesman for the union, this could add additional dangers. . . . I was a native-born citizen. In addition I was well known to quite a large section of the prospective recruits. I had been a candidate of the Communist Party
for U. S. Senator in 1928 and was therefore known quite widely
in several important sectors of the state . . . We came to agreement, after long discussion and consideration of the local and
state political climate."

Also to be noted is the salutary fact that Ray and Carl always acted as a team. Neither was given to strutting about
as an individual star or posturing as the fount of all wisdom.
Both were serious revolutionists, organization men, who knew
how to teach younger leaders by precept and example.

Under their guidance a broadening leadership team was
gradually forged. In the opening stage of the Teamster campaign the team was reinforced by Grant and Miles Dunne,
both party members who worked in the coal yards, as did
Ray and Carl. Key supporting roles were played by two other
party members in the trade unions: Oscar Coover, Sr., a skilled
electrician in the building trades; and C. R. Hedlund, a loco-
motive engineer on the Northwestern railway. Soon to be added
to the team were militant young workers who began to develop
as leaders during the struggle in the coal industry.

The campaign was opened in that particular industry for
specific reasons: Communist League members were employed
there; the coal yards were the strategic place to start the action because of the subzero Minnesota winters. If the yards
could be effectively closed down in a strike, the employers
would be unable to sit tight in the hope of starving the strikers
into submission. Such a course was more or less excluded
by the fact that people would have to be supplied with coal
during the cold winter weather. This circumstance was accen-
tuated by the fact that under the depressed economic conditions of the day many people could afford to buy only a small
quantity of fuel at one time. It was, therefore, possible that
a well-timed and properly conducted strike could win a relatively quick settlement in the union's favor, even though it
might be only a partial victory.

This, of course, would have to be accomplished in the face

of stiff employer resistance. if the effort succeeded, the stage would be set to organize the rest of the trucking industry. In the process, the paralysis that afflicted the AFL unions generally could be overcome and the whole town could be organized.

It would take a class war to achieve these objectives and the outcome depended on the capacity of the Communist League to play a key role in guiding and inspiring the whole movement. The lingering effects in the Minnesota AFL of a previous period of radical influence could be counted on as a favorable factor. In Minneaplis there were numerous trade unionists who retained memories of radical unionism in the past. Some considered themselves socialists in a loose sense. Others had kept alive a spark of militancy from their IWW days. Once a real strike struggle got underway in the city, many of them could be expected to rally to the cause like old warhorses responding to the sound of a bugle.

Development of the struggle required the surmounting of bureaucratic obstacles in the Central Labor Union and the Teamsters Joint Council. Within Local 574 this problem centered on Cliff Hall, who worked hand and glove with the rest of the bureaucrats sitting on top of the city's unions. These worthies had somehow existed in their posts for years without winning a strike. For that shortcoming they smugly blamed the workers. Steeped as they were in collaboration with "fair" employers, they could be expected to be hostile toward the projected strike action. Yet it would not do to open a frontal attack on the bureaucrats. Such a step would give the mistaken impression that the main objective of the campaign was to win union posts. As that would hamper the organizing drive, it was necessary to develop a flanking tactic.

The key to such a tactic lay in a contradiction faced by the union bureaucrats. In their fundamental outlook they were oriented toward collaboration with the capitalists, but they were of no value to the ruling class unless they had a base from which to operate in the unions. To maintain such a base they had to deliver something for the workers. In the campaign about to begin, however, they would be put up against leadership responsibilities that they couldn't meet. Thus the indicated tactic was to aim the workers' fire straight at the employers and catch the union bureaucrats in the middle. If they didn't react positively, they would stand discredited.

Another factor to be considered was the Minnesota Farmer-

Labor Party. Based on an alliance of trade unions and farmers' organizations, the party had been launched in the aftermath of World War I. As it gained momentum a number of
supporters also came forward from within the urban middle
class. Thanks largely to the role of left-wing trade unionists,
the founding of this independent political movement marked
a break from earlier attempts in the region to capture a capitalist party. Although the FLP put up candidates against
both the Democrats and Republicans, its program was limited essentially to demands for reform of the capitalist system. As a result, confused patterns of class political consciousness developed among the party's rank-and-file supporters.
Organizationally these forces were drawn together through
a federation of local clubs, which existed in city wards and
rural communities. In addition, trade unions constituted a
principal component of the federation.

From the outset the Farmer-Labor Party candidates for public office tended to assume control over the party. Their primary aim was to get themselves elected, and they played fast
and loose with principles to achieve that goal. The party's
first major victory was the election of a U. S. Senator and
a couple of congressmen in 1922. Then in 1930 it captured
the governorship of the state, making it the only party of its
kind ever to win such a seat of power in this country. The
year 1933 saw the FLP governor begin his second term in
office. In the state legislature at that time the FLP made a
bloc with liberal capitalist politicians to control the lower house,
but the senate remained predominantly conservative.

It should be noted in passing that the Communist Party
had played a role in the emergence of the Farmer-Labor Party. Then in 1928 the CP decided to run its own candidate
against the FLP nominee for U. S. Senator. Ray Dunne, who
for years had been secretary of the 12th Ward FLP Club in
Minneapolis, was chosen by the CP as its candidate. This
brought about his expulsion from the Farmer-Labor Party,
and soon thereafter he was thrown out of the Communist Party on charges of "Trotskyism."

Because of its base among the workers and farmers, the
Farmer-Labor Party had a dual nature. In contrast to the un-
principled political conniving of its candidates on the electoral
arena, the party was also a mass movement with a membership that took part in farmers' struggles and in trade-union
activities. For one thing this meant that its representatives in

public office had to show sympathy toward the trade unions in conflicts with the employers. Since many unorganized workers supported the party at the ballot box, these officeholders also had to favor unionization of such workers as both a right and a necessity.

Floyd B. Olson was the FLP candidate who had been elected in 1930 as governor of the state, and reelected in 1932. A lawyer with some early trade-union experience, he had previously been county attorney of Hennepin County in which Minneapolis is situated. Olson considered himself bigger than the movement he represented. This led him to act more or less as a free-agent politically, making self-serving deals with politicians in the capitalist parties.

So far as the Communist League's objectives were concerned, Olson's presence in the governor's chair was both good and bad at the same time. On the plus side was the fact that the governor, who had based his political career on the FLP, couldn't afford to act openly as a strikebreaker. Instead he would have to give some measure of open support to a unionization campaign. On the minus side was the expectation that in a showdown fight with the employers, Olson and the trade-union bureaucrats would try to take over the leadership of the union forces.

This was a real danger because the governor was a persuasive person, clever in his actions. He was respected in the union ranks and no union official had ever dared to cross him. To the Communist League leaders this meant that any question of sympathy strikes by other unions in support of a Local 574 walkout would have to be carefully handled. Otherwise the way could be opened for Olson to step in and take command by way of the officials in other unions. It was therefore necessary to build up Local 574's strength so that, even in the toughest going, it could make a strong showing on its own against the enemy class.

In confronting the employers, Local 574 would be up against the Citizens Alliance. This was an employer organization that took its inspiration from the crushing of a 1918 streetcar strike through the use of wartime home guards. It was dominated by the wealthiest and most powerful local capitalists. In matters of labor relations they rode herd over the smaller-fry employers of whom there were some 800 in the organization. The Citizens Alliance tolerated no defections from its policy, and reprisals were taken against employers who violated its labor code. It maintained a full-time staff, had stool pigeons planted in the trade unions, got full cooperation from city hall, and had the police at its service. The enemy class was well organized for strikebreaking, and it was extremely cocky.

All in all, the projected trade-union campaign was a big undertaking with many pitfalls and dangers. Nevertheless, sound reasons existed for setting it into motion. There was also good cause to begin on a note of optimism. In the coal yards, where the first steps would be taken, workers with radical backgrounds could be counted upon to help the project along.

The Opening Wedge

An attempt to get the Local 574 campaign started was first made in the winter of 1930-31. Carl Skoglund and Miles Dunne were sent into the union to feel out the possibilities of promoting a drive to unionize the coal industry. Before long internal gossip was spread about Carl being a "radical troublemaker" and the business agent refused to accept dues from him. Miles, who was less well known than Carl, was not bothered, but he had to take it easy inside the union in order to be there later on if things should take a turn for the better. Meantime, some way had to be found to overcome this initial setback.

A more circumspect approach to the task was set into motion, beginning in the DeLaittre-Dixon Fuel yard. Ray, Miles, and Grant Dunne, along with Carl Skoglund and Martin Soderberg, were employed there and they initiated the voluntary organizing committee that I was to join two years later. A careful method of procedure had to be devised in order to avoid victimizations on the job. It was not possible to issue leaflets and hold open meetings as could have been done through Local 574. Instead individual workers would have to be sounded out in a careful way.

Although the process would be a slow one at the outset, objective conditions indicated that gradual headway could be made. Tactically, the rate of development had to be considered secondary to a cumulative record of progress. As additional forces were thus gathered, they in turn would give fresh impetus to the campaign, and at the proper stage the workers could be led into action.

The first big break came when DeLaittre-Dixon merged with a few smaller yards to form an expanded firm known as Fuel Distributors. With a larger body of workers brought together in the new setup, improved prospects were at hand for win-

ning support for the unionization project. Among the new
supporters gained through the change were Harry DeBoer
and Kelly Postal, who were later to play important roles in
Local 574. C. B. Carlson, a worker at a nearby yard, also
volunteered to help. This reinforcement of the organizational
staff enabled the recruiting campaign to gain steadily in momentum.

A stage had now been reached where it was important to
bring the prounion forces together for a collective discussion
and recruitment session. The problem was how to swing it
when there was no official union framework available and
the bosses would be quick to take reprisals if they got wind
of what was going on. A unique solution was found. Utilizing
his position as weighmaster for the purpose, Ray Dunne got
the employer's approval of a plan to hold a beer bust for
employees only. Pointing out that the bosses held such affairs
among themselves, Ray argued that an employee gathering
would be a good way to build up "company morale." The
employer was so impressed with the plan that he not only
okayed it—he paid the hall rent and bought the beer. The
affair was a big success that gave the union drive a substantial forward push.

When word of the beer bust got around in the Communist
League, criticisms were made by a few armchair strategists
who were stronger in book learning than they were in class
struggle know-how. They hinted darkly that a company union
was in danger of being formed, which meant a setup where-
in the boss had direct influence. The foolish charge stemmed
from the report that the employer had financed the beer bust,
a matter that the workers involved had thought quite humor-
ous.

This small episode demonstrates how important it is to be
careful about making sweeping tactical judgments from afar.
In such circumstances too little is usually known about the
complex factors involved to justify forming a categorical opinion. If it is a slow-moving situation, long and fruitless argument can ensue without an early opportunity to subject
the opposing views to the test of events. Fortunately, in the
case of the coal yard action, the tempo was picking up and
it didn't take long for the beer bust tactic to be proven valid
for the given specific purposes.

It does not follow, however, that use of an employer to un-
wittingly help along a trade-union campaign is a device to

be applied generally. Such an interpretation would imply that the tactic in itself was viewed as a clever and quick way to organize workers. Nothing could be further from the facts. The beer bust was arranged simply as a unique solution to an unusual problem.

Things continued to move along reasonably well until Ray Dunne was suddenly fired from his job at Fuel Distributors. Fears immediately arose that the employers were opening a counterattack in an effort to scotch the unionization campaign. However, that did not turn out to be the reason for his discharge. As a spokesman for the Communist League, he occasionally made public speeches on political topics, some of which had been mentioned in the press. "This embarrasses us," the employer said, "and we must let you go."

Ray's discharge led to talk among some militants in the yard about organizing a protest strike. The situation was carefully discussed in the party fraction, and it was decided to dissuade the workers from taking such a step. Spring had come and the coal season was about over. The action could take place in only one yard and it would involve the case of a weighmaster, a position that was looked upon as semi-supervisory. After considering these factors, the workers generally came to an understanding that it was best to let the matter ride. Since no other job was available, Ray and his family had to go on public relief which thrust them into very hard times.

Despite this setback the campaign moved ahead, experiencing further ups and downs along the way. By the fall of 1933 the situation had developed to the point where things were ripe for a qualitative leap forward. Several objective factors were operating to make this possible. For one thing deplorable conditions within the industry had imposed upon the workers a strong need to find some means of defending their interests. My own problems as a coal worker, described previously, were more or less typical of those faced by all workers in the industry. Low wages and long hours made it bad enough, even when one had steady work as a yardman or a driver of a company truck. For some workers things were even worse.

Most firms had a policy of keeping surplus trucks on hand by hiring individually owned rigs. A commission was paid by the ton for coal delivered in this manner. Covering both the driver's labor and the use of his truck, it was figured at pea-

nut rates. Carrymen were underpaid by the ton for toting
heavy baskets of coal on their shoulder when it could not
be delivered directly from the truck to the bin. Sometimes they
had to climb two or three flights of stairs with their burden.

Since commission drivers and carrymen went payless between deliveries, earnings in these categories were so low that
some workers had to seek supplementary public relief. When
they were idle they sat at the coal yard in a little heated shack
aptly called a "doghouse." Since there was usually a card game
and a lot of talking going on, it was a good place for union
organizers to get in some points.

Wiseacres of the day spoke pontifically about the "passivity"
of the working class, never understanding that the seeming
docility of the workers at a given time is a relative thing.
If workers are more or less holding their own in daily life
and expecting that they can get ahead slowly, they won't tend
to radicalize. Things are different when they are losing ground
and the future looks precarious to them. Then a change begins
to occur in their attitude, which is not always immediately
apparent. The tinder of discontent begins to pile up. Any spark
can light it, and once lit, the fire can spread rapidly.

In Minneapolis the flames were bound to become widespread
because it was not only the coal workers who were being driven
toward action to correct an increasingly intolerable situation.
Conditions were bad throughout the entire trucking industry.
Wages were as low as ten dollars and rarely above eighteen
dollars for a workweek ranging from fifty-four to ninety hours.

To cite specific cases, drivers for wholesale grocery houses
received fifty-five to sixty-five dollars a month for which they
put in fifty-four hours a week with nothing extra for overtime. Workers employed at jobs inside the grocery warehouses
got ten to fifteen dollars a month less. Employees of the mul-
tiplicity of firms in the wholesale fruit and vegetable market
were paid as little as ten dollars a week to start. If an old-
timer earned as much as eighteen to twenty dollars he was
considered lucky. They worked from as early as 3:00 A. M.
to as late as 6:00 P. M., six days a week. If a worker complained, he was fired and the Citizens Alliance employment
office supplied a new hand.

Drivers operating the big fleet of taxis owned by the Yellow Cab Company worked on a commission basis which
brought them six to eight dollars for eighty-four-hour week.
Many had to obtain public relief in order to get by. All the

workers in every category had to accept whatever job conditions the employers imposed, and deep-seated grievances were widespread among them as a result. Once an effective union struggle got underway, the bulk of these workers, who stood outside the union movement, would be ready to move swiftly into organized action. The tycoons who ran the Citizens Alliance had sown the wind and they were about to reap the whirlwind.

Another objective factor impinging upon the Minneapolis scene was the general working-class upsurge then beginning to take place throughout the country. Seeking help from the official labor movement to defend their class interests, workers were pouring into the AFL in growing numbers. During 1933 a mounting wave of strikes developed nationally. This trend arose primarily because of low pay, long hours and a general feeling of insecurity. It got further impetus from one aspect of Roosevelt's "New Deal" which had been in operation since the spring of the year. Section 7(a) of the newly adopted National Industrial Recovery Act (NRA) purportedly guaranteed the workers the "right to organize." This official declaration helped along the process of unionization, even though the workers were to find themselves mistaken in their belief that the capitalist government would actually protect their rights.

At root the NRA was devised for the benefit of the capitalist class. To stimulate production for profit, Roosevelt had adopted an "easy money" policy leading to what was called the "sixty-cent dollar." The resulting climb in prices struck a new blow at the workers who were already suffering the dire effects of economic depression. As a consequence, organized labor intensified its pressure for government assistance through wage and hour laws. To sidestep labor's demands, the NRA provided for self-organization of "fair competition" among employers who would voluntarily set minimum-wage rates and maximum hours. To give them a free hand, antitrust laws were suspended. NRA labor codes for each industry were thereby decided by the employers alone. The workers had no voice in the matter.

Regional Labor Boards were set up by the Federal government, staffed by employers' agents and "labor statesmen." Their chief function was to prevent strikes by whatever means possible. When a work stoppage took place despite their efforts, they were to "mediate" a settlement as quickly as they could. In practice this meant trying to get the workers back on the job with a vague promise of subsequent action on their demands through some form of continued intervention by the Labor Board. The whole scheme operated in favor of the bosses, and brought the workers many bitter experiences.

Hailing Roosevelt as labor's saviour, the top AFL officials made a no-strike agreement with the NRA administrators. They also agreed to a clause in the NRA labor code recognizing company unions as legitimate organizations. This entitled such boss-controlled setups to bid for certification as the workers' bargaining agent in union-representation elections conducted by the Labor Board.

In Minneapolis, however, the Citizens Alliance leaders took the view that the NRA didn't go far enough in their favor on the collective-bargaining issue. A directive was issued to the employers of the city that no union whatever was needed, in any form, for bargaining with their labor force. Workers should be urged, the Citizens Alliance said, to "bargain" with the employer as individuals concerning the terms of their employment. This hard-nosed employer policy caused the local AFL officials to lean all the more heavily upon the Regional Labor Board.

A problem resulted for the insurgent workers, especially the younger militants who spearheaded the radicalization. Their youthfulness freed them from the inhibiting effects of earlier labor defeats and they moved toward battle with the bosses as though they were inventing something new. It followed, however, that they were inexperienced and didn't know just how to conduct the fight. This made them vulnerable to AFL misleaders trained in the Gompers school. A saving factor existed in the workers' objective need to find leaders with a correct policy and the fighting ability to carry it out. To meet this need, the help of a revolutionary socialist party was required.

As the political vanguard of the class, the revolutionary party constitutes a bridge in historic consciousness for the workers. It absorbs the lessons of the class struggle, victories as well as defeats, preserving them as part of its revolutionary heritage. The party's cadres are the mechanism through which this "class memory" is infused into labor struggles on the given contemporary scene. The Communist League cadres could fulfill this role in the trucking industry if they could link themselves with the militant workers through the trade-union movement. In their approach to this problem the comrades made a distinction between formal and actual leadership.

Holding an official post does not automatically make one a leader. A semblance of leadership authority can be maintained for a time through bureaucratic abuse of official powers, but in the long run one must actually meet the responsibilities of a given post or a leadership void will be created. In the latter case someone else can step into the void and begin to exercise actual leadership authority without necessarily holding an official post. A contradictory situation develops, the outcome of which has to be determined by the course of events. In the end the more competent leader, as proven through performance, can wind up with the official authority as well.

It follows that the ultimate gaining of such official authority marks the end of what has been a war on two fronts. The central object all along will have been to lead an effective struggle against the employers. When incompetent union officials hold formal authority it becomes necessary to fight them at the same time. Once the incompetents have been replaced in formal authority by capable leaders, however, the way is clear to concentrate on the struggle against the enemy class.

The Communist League leaders realized that, if it became necessary in the case of Local 574, the whole executive board would have to be confronted head on. Yet it would have been unwise for them to proceed as though this was the only available course of action. As every good tactician knows, it is important to seek a way to split the opposition. A way to do so was found with respect to the Local 574 problem by exploiting a situation common to all union bureaucracies.

These formations are not as wholly monolithic as might appear at first sight. The most hidebound component is at the very top. Under that top crust there are layers of lesser officials who are closer to the union ranks and more subject to influence by the workers. Although these lesser officials are under pressure from the top to act as police against the union ranks, they are sometimes disinclined to do so when the workers are up in arms against the employers. How they may act in a given situation depends upon the direction from which the strongest wind is blowing at the time.

In Local 574 a means of developing the desired tactic arose

from the fact that Miles Dunne had been able to continue inside the union since joining it in 1931. During the interval he
had struck up a close acquaintance with the local's president,
William S. Brown, who showed interest in the idea of a general
organizing drive. Bill Brown, who was in his middle thirties,
had worked for years as both a teamster and a truck driver
in the transfer industry, which had to do mostly with hauling
freight. He had held the presidency of Local 574 for ten years
and in 1932 he was made organizer of the Teamsters Joint
Council.

Bill was a fighter by nature and a gifted speaker, one of the
best mass agitators I ever heard. As an activist in the Farmer-
Labor Party, he was somewhat above average in political
consciousness, even though he lacked a revolutionary understanding of the class struggle. A career as an AFL official
was open to him and he might have gone on in that direction
if the campaign launched by the Communist League hadn't
affected his life.

As it was, Bill's sound class instincts came to the fore. He
wanted to give the bosses a real battle and he welcomed help
from people who knew how to organize the fight. Within Local
574 Bill won support for such a course from George Frosig,
the vice-president. However, the other five members of the executive board were unable to lift themselves out of the mire of
business unionism. They remained under the influence of Cliff
Hall, the business agent, who sat as an ex-officio member of
the board and opposed the organizing project. The door had
been opened only a crack; it would take the pressure of the
coal workers to push it wide open.

The needed push came from the volunteer organizing committee, which began to mushroom in the fall of 1933. It broke
the resistance of the executive-board majority. Hall became
isolated within the Local 574 officialdom and he had to go
along with the organizing drive in coal. When the demands
upon the coal employers had been drawn up and ratified by
the union membership, Hall submitted them to Tobin for approval. Tobin's reply of January 6, 1934, showed that he had
sharpened up his no-strike line since his 1930 exchange of letters with Hall.

"I trust you understand the law of the International Union,"
Tobin wrote, "which is that the approval of a wage scale is
not the approval of a strike, or does not give you the right
to strike even if there is no agreement with your employers

on the contract. It is your duty to proceed to negotiate, and if after negotiations end or are broken up by the employers and you can reach no agreement, it is then your duty under the law [of Tobin's making — FD] to offer to arbitrate the questions at issue, or the differences between you. If the employers refuse to arbitrate and there is no other alternative, you may proceed to consider the question of a strike. In order to comply with the International laws and obtain sanction of a strike, you must report the entire proceedings at a regular or special meeting of your organization, explaining every detail as to the conferences, etc.

"After the discussion on same has taken place you will then proceed to ballot as to whether the men want to strike. The question should be answered 'yes' or 'no.' Blank slips of paper, numbered, should be passed amongst the members and the vote should be taken without any intimidation on the part of the members. When the vote is taken it is necessary to have two-thirds of the members present vote in the affirmative, or in favor of the strike, or by using the word 'yes,' in order to obtain sanction of the International Executive Board. As soon as this is done, if there is a Joint Council in your district it is necessary for you then to submit the matter for approval to the Joint Council. When the Joint Council gives their sanction you will then proceed and ask the International Union for its sanction, giving them the facts in the case, or in other words the differences between yourselves and the employers. You must then wait until the International Executive Board has had a chance to vote on same. If you go on strike before you receive the sanction of the International Executive Board you will not receive any benefits whatsoever from the International Union."

Obviously it would take a near miracle to get Tobin's official sanction for a strike. If the employers won't negotiate a contract, he decreed, try to get them to arbitrate. Only if they reject that step should a strike vote be taken, and that should be done in a way calculated to curb militancy and magnify conservative hesitations within the union's ranks. "A strike is a serious situation," Tobin said in another part of his letter, "and should not be attempted unless there is at least 75% of the men working at the craft organized and willing to answer the call. It is also very well to remember that a strike does not last usually for only two or three days . . ."

If in spite of everything the local membership voted to strike, there remained the obstacles of a Teamsters Joint Council endorsement and final approval from Tobin himself. Failure to observe this procedure meant that no strike benefits in the form of financial aid to the striking workers would be paid by the International. As later events will show, Tobin was not above publicly attacking an embattled union for actions which he deemed to be "illegal."

With the aid of Brown and Frosig the volunteer committee bypassed Tobin's procedure which would have brought the whole campaign to a grinding halt. A strike decision was made by Local 574; through Brown's influence some backing was won in the Teamsters Joint Council; and without further ado the local went into action. In accordance with sound tactical methods, plans were made to overcome stiff employer resistance, even though there was reason to assume that a well-conducted strike could catch the bosses unprepared. Tactically, it is always better to be prepared for the worst variant and not have to face it, than it is to expect the best breaks and suddenly run into unexpected obstacles.

A broad strike committee was organized to assume command of the picketing. Before the walkout began, mimeographed picketing instructions were prepared, along with maps showing the location of all coal yards.

The strike hit the industry with a bang. Characterized by militant mass picketing from the outset, the whole operation was both audacious and efficient. The pickets, mainly young workers in their first labor struggle, reinforced the careful planning by experienced leaders with courageous actions during which they came up with some innovations of their own. Development and use of cruising picket squads was an outstanding example of the rank-and-file ingenuity.

While all this was being prepared, Hall had reported the situation to Tobin. On February 5, 1934 he received a telegraphed reply from Tobin's assistant, John M. Gillespie. "You will have to write full particulars as to what you want to strike for," he said, "also the number of men that will be affected. Would advise that you wait until Brother Geary [Tobin's general organizer in the area — FD] gets back to your district before going further with the strike. Your telegram gives practically no information, only that you want endorsement. You can appeal your case to the Labor Board in Washington and try to have them force the coal dealers to meet you."

Just as the walkout was beginning on February 7 Gillespie mailed another communication to Hall. "As these men have not been members of your organization for six months," he ruled on Tobin's behalf, "strike endorsement, including financial benefits, cannot be granted, as in accordance with our laws men must be members of our organization six months or over in order to be entitled to strike benefits." By the time this letter arrived in Minneapolis the strike was about to be settled.

The whirlwind action had indeed caught the bosses unprepared. They were put in a further bind by the frigid cold wave that accompanied the walkout and led to stiff public pressure for fuel deliveries. With the yards tied up tight, the employers had to make a settlement which brought the workers limited material gains. Most importantly, however, they had been compelled to recognize the union. Even though the recognition came indirectly through the Labor Board, it marked a fundamental departure from the open-shop precepts of the Citizens Alliance.

For the first time in many years a strike had been won in Minneapolis. Electrified by the victory, union members throughout the city gained self-confidence and thousands of unorganized workers lifted their eyes toward the union movement with a new sense of hope. The stage was now set for the main conflict, and both sides began to gird for the showdown that was soon to begin.

General Mobilization

Life itself was verifying the Communist League's trade-union policy. Its strategy and tactics had enabled conscious revolutionists to unite with the workers in an effective mass action. Despite weaknesses in the official union leadership, the coal workers had been able to test their organized strength and win a contest with the employers. They were learning to have confidence in themselves as a class. They also began to absorb some basic lessons about the class struggle as these were revealed in the heat of battle.

Illusions about the police began to be dispelled when the workers found the whole force on the side of the bosses. There were comparable experiences with the Labor Board. When the union demands were first presented the board's role had been simply to transmit the employers' arrogant refusal to negotiate. Then it sought to postpone the strike beyond the cold season to the union's disadvantage. In the collective-bargaining election held after the strike, the board ordered that the vote be taken yard by yard, instead of on an industry-wide basis as the union demanded. The obvious intent was to help employers weasel out of recognizing the union in at least a few yards if they could. Though none of these capers did the employers much good, they did help teach the workers whose side the "neutral" Labor Board was really on.

A correct strategic and tactical course had made these results possible. To transform such a possibility into reality, however, it had been necessary for the Communist League members to conduct themselves in action as a disciplined combat force. Within the union the party fraction functioned as a cohesive unit, harmoniously united in carrying out party policy. Intimate contact was maintained between the fraction and the local party branch.

The results obtained through this disciplined course of action gave a big new lift to party morale and efforts were stepped up to recruit new members into the Communist League. Toward that end a public meeting was held after the strike to discuss the need for a new revolutionary party to replace the politically bankrupt Stalinist movement. It proved to be one of the biggest gatherings of its kind in the city in years. Most notable was the presence of a considerable number of coal workers, some of whom were to join the party relatively soon.

Meantime the Communist League was mapping out plans for continuation of the trade-union campaign. The victory in the coal industry had been uniquely important, since it did a lot to overcome existing obstacles to a larger mass mobilization for the next action. Many workers elsewhere in the trucking industry harbored resentment over the way the unionization campaigns of the past, none of which ever brought any meaningful results, had been handled. It was more than a case of once bitten, twice shy. They had little confidence in the weak craft unions that had a long record of lost strikes.

Now, however, the workers saw the first signs of a new approach. Unlike the piecemeal nibbling of the past, the whole boss setup in coal had been struck, with all the coal workers involved in the struggle. The employers had been forced to recognize the union while it was on strike. This fact was dramatized by the unprecedented appearance of Local 574 buttons on coal drivers after the strike, as they made deliveries throughout the city. Favorable changes in attitude toward the union were bound to follow among workers throughout the whole trucking industry.

The first step in taking advantage of the improved situation had to be the shaping of the necessary leadership to carry out a general organizing drive. New forces for the purpose were at hand among the young militants who came to the fore during the coal strike. They were capable recruiters who, as they campaigned, would also be on the lookout for new volunteer organizers. More than that — in the next strike they would make up the hard core around which a broader combat leadership could be formed. If these campaigners were to function effectively they had to have a reasonably free hand.

The indicated device for this was to upgrade the informal organizing committee developed in the coal actions to the status of an official union body. This was readily accomplished at a general membership meeting of Local 574 because coal

workers now predominated in the union and they tended to
look upon the organizing committee as their real leadership.
A passage in the minutes of its first meeting records the
composition of the new body: "The Voluntary Organizing Committee met in the office of the General Drivers, 614 First Ave.
No., Friday, March 16, at 8 PM. Committee consisted of the
following volunteer members, together with all of the members
of the executive board: Harry DeBoer, Floyd O'Berg, C. Quick,
Pete Bove, M. Dunne, C. Skoglund, F. Dobbs, G. Dunne, A.
Brace, Chris Moe, S. Fredericks, E. Sunde, W. Thompson,
S. Baumgartner, C. Nelson." The executive-board members
to which the minutes refer were at that time: W. S. Brown,
G. Frosig, H. Esler, S. Haskell, W. Gray, J. Nolan, and M.
Hork. The business agent, C. Hall, sat in ex officio at committee meetings, as he did at executive-board sessions.
As the minutes note, the full executive board attended the
meeting. Hall seemed to have in mind official monitoring of
the organizing committee but that wasn't exactly the way things
were to work out. Actually a new stage of dual leadership
control was being developed. The strength of the organizing
committee in the union ranks was about to be counterposed
to the formal authority of the executive board. In the process
the volunteer organizers would gain added weight from the
solid support they were given by Brown and Frosig, both
of whom were members of the executive board. Further advantage derived from the formal status now accorded to the
organizing committee by decision of the union membership.
These combined factors enabled the committee to bypass the
executive board on some matters and to force it into line on
others, according to the given situation. In short, the committee became a sort of special executive authority heading
up the work of the volunteer organizers who were to grow
quite rapidly in number.
Through this specific form of rank-and-file democracy, bureaucratic obstacles to the organizing drive were overcome,
but another leadership problem remained unsolved. Negotiations with employers were still largely in the hands of incompetent union officials. This meant that gains won on the picket
line could still be lost at the conference table. Even though
nothing much could be done about it as matters stood at the
time, the problem required close attention with a view toward
taking effective action at the first opportunity.
Changes already taking place in the leadership structure

were reflected in the nature and scope of the organizing drive. The contrast between the old and the new was illustrated by differing views set forth in joint meetings of the organizing committee and executive board. Hall and his cronies, who thought in terms of old-time campaigns conducted by Local 574, considered what had happened in coal a fluke. Their idea was to peddle a few leaflets, bring in some new dues-payers, and keep two sets of books on the project so Tobin wouldn't get any per capita tax on those who dropped away after a time. In fact one executive-board member didn't even want to spend money for leaflets. "They know where we are," he said of the unorganized workers, "if they want to join the union, let them come to the hall and sign up."

The organizing committee had a different concept. Its aim was to build a strong union force to battle the bosses throughout the trucking industry as had already been done in coal. A partial list of the sections into which the industry was subdivided for campaign purposes will give an idea of the scope of the operation. These included transfer companies; building material firms; wholesale houses handling fruit, produce, and groceries; package delivery outfits; fleet drivers in the taxi field; the delivery end of department and furniture stores; oil companies, including filling stations; oxygen and acetylene suppliers, and others. Employees whom the committee set out to organize included drivers, helpers, yard workers, platform hands, shipping-room employees, packers, and other inside workers on jobs loosely connected with trucking services. Not only did the organizing committee ignore Tobin's dictum that the workers be divided into separate locals according to the commodities they handled; it also passed beyond the narrow jurisdictional limits set by him for the IBT as a whole.

This had broader significance for the future of the entire Teamsters Union. *For the first time a Teamsters local was about to move toward the industrial form of organization, taking all the workers in a given enterprise into a single union.*

Just as the union campaign was getting under way it received an unintentional boost from the coal bosses. Having been unable to break the February strike, they set out to defeat the union another way. Spring was coming and the coal season would soon be running out. The employers decided to weed out the union militants by hitting them first in the seasonal layoffs that were soon due. In this way, they figured, the rest of the workers could be intimidated, and by

the time business picked up again in the fall open-shop conditions could be restored in the industry.

The scheme boomeranged. A life-and-death question was
posed for the workers hit by discriminatory layoffs. If they
didn't help to push the union forward, it was obvious that
they would never get back into the coal yards; and other jobs
were very scarce in those depression times. On the other hand,
if the union's summer campaign succeeded, it would take only
a mopping-up operation in the fall to entrench Local 574
in the coal industry and put the victimized workers back on
the job. Consequently there was a sudden increase in voluntary union organizers.

I was among those who got the ax in coal. Pitching into
the union campaign full time, I was teamed up with Carl
Skoglund on an organizing assignment. Working with him
proved to be a golden opportunity for a new Communist
League member to learn a lot. In addition to what he taught
me about union organizing, we also found time to talk about
revolutionary politics. One of Carl's foremost talents was his
ability to teach young people the lessons he had learned. A
Marxist worker with a high level of intellectual development,
he understood the importance of theory and its use as a guide
for action. He started me on a reading course in Marxist classics; then we would discuss what I had read and he would
patiently explain points I didn't understand. The experience
was twice rich for me because, in addition to having a capable teacher, my lessons were enhanced by the intensive class
struggle in which I was participating.

In the union work, organizing teams like ours went to ga-
rages, docks, warehouses, market areas, everywhere in the
trucking industry. Wherever we went we found the workers
waiting for us, and union recruitment proceeded with accel-
erating momentum. A class was organized to train volunteer
speakers who then appeared before meetings of other unions
to explain Local 574's campaign and ask their support. Although not all the officials in other unions were happy about
these visits, Local 574 speakers were usually well received
by the memberships. Efforts were also made to get publicity
for the campaign in *Labor Review,* the official organ of the
AFL Central Labor Union. Through these combined activities the Local 574 campaign soon became a prime topic of
conversation within the city's working class and most everybody watched to see what would happen next.

In their recruiting work the organizing teams not only talked about joining the union; they also raised the question of demands to be made upon the employers. No greater authority on the subject could be found than the workers on the job. Collectively they have rich practical knowledge of the industry in which they are employed; they know all the employer's tricks and about the only secret he can keep from them is how much profit he is raking off from their labor. Meetings were held with each group of workers to formulate specific demands for their particular section of the trucking industry. They made the decisions on all items relating to wages, hours, and working conditions. The organizing committee simply added special clauses on points such as union recognition, job protection, grievance procedures, and comparable matters.

Wage demands, as formulated by the workers themselves, varied from eighteen to thirty-five dollars a week, according to job classifications. These ranged from tomato strippers in the produce market to drivers of heavy hauling equipment. Demands on hours called for a workweek varying from forty to forty-eight hours, with premium pay for overtime. Job conditions against which the workers were rebelling were eloquently described by some of the demands: no split shifts; garage-to-garage time; guarantee of a half day's pay when called to report for work; regular brake tests at company expense; no chiseling on pay by juggling job classifications; workers not to be liable for loss of, or damage to, merchandise; full wages to be paid each week on a regular pay day.

With the completion of this step in the organizing drive the time had come to turn toward the showdown with the bosses. Quite a fighting force was being put together for the purpose. A leadership with a firm class-struggle program was gradually gaining command within the union. It was pressing vigorously for rank-and-file control over all union affairs; close ties were developing between the membership and the organizing committee; and in shaping the union demands, the workers had written their own ticket. With these strong incentives, virtually every union member became a volunteer recruiter and a front line fighter in the Local 574 campaign.

Careful organizational preparation had cleared the way for a public demonstration of the union's growth—which could have several good effects. A mass assembly would give the workers an image of their developing strength. Those experiencing doubts and hesitations about the union could be fa-

vorably influenced. The stage would be set publicly for pre-
sentation of the union's demands on the employers; and Local
574 would be shown to represent the workers. For this occasion the organizing committee proposed to rent the Shubert
Theater, a downtown entertainment center designed for stage
productions that was frequently used by other big organizations.

There was resistance to the proposal, as was noted in the
March 21 minutes of a joint meeting of the organizing committee and the executive board: "Report of committee on securing theater and speakers. Brother Brown reporting, that committee recommends the securing of Shubert Theater which can
probably be rented for $66, including two stage hands. . . .
Brother Hall reporting for the executive board, that it was
in favor of not spending much money at this time and recommended that the number one hall at Labor Headquarters be
secured for mass meeting instead of Shubert Theater. Brother
Gray also spoke in support of Brother Hall's position. Brothers Brown, Skoglund and M. Dunne spoke on the necessity
of securing a larger hall. . . . Brother M. Dunne proposed
that a collection be taken up at mass meeting to defray expenses. Brother Brown proposed that other unions contribute
toward this expense." Hall's objections were overridden and
the Shubert was rented for the mass meeting.

The organizing committee also started a pressure campaign
to line up Govenor Olson as a speaker at the meeting. This
was done for two main reasons: advance publicity listing the
governor as a speaker would help in getting a big turnout
for the meeting; and if Olson addressed the workers, he would
have to go on record in support of the union campaign. The
governor tried to duck the assignment but so much pressure
was put on him that he finally agreed to speak. A leaflet was
then distributed throughout the industry announcing that Olson
would address the workers on "The Right to Organize." The
workers were also informed that speakers from Local 574
would outline a definite program of organization for their
approval.

When the meeting was called to order on Sunday afternoon,
April 15, 1934, the big theater was packed. Grant Dunne made
a report for the organizing committee. Bill Brown and Miles
Dunne gave fighting talks that really whipped up the workers'
enthusiasm. I, too, had been assigned to give what would be
my first public speech, and the prospect of facing that big

crowd scared me stiff. Before the rally I had asked Carl Skoglund for help. "When you get up there just be what you are," he counseled, "a young worker with family responsibilities in hard times. Most of those in the audience will be young workers like yourself. Just describe what you think needs to be done and they will feel that you are speaking for them." I followed Carl's advice as best I could and managed to get by.

Govenor Olson did not appear at the meeting. Instead he put himself on record in a way that was even better for the union. His private secretary, Vince Day, came to the gathering and brought with him a letter signed by the govenor. Day, who called himself a philosophical anarchist, first made a rather militant talk on his own behalf. Then he read Olson's message, dated April 13, to the assembled workers, after which he handed it over to Brown for the union file.

Key passages in the governor's letter stated: "The union idea, and I don't mean the company union, is fundamentally sound. . . . Vested interests have gone the limit in their attempt to defeat the union idea because they knew that complete unionism meant the end of their reign of exploitation of the working man and woman. However, labor has weathered gun fire, injunctions and prosecution by malicious propaganda and has built up a network of unions that forms the most powerful single organization in our country. . . . It is my counsel, if you wish to accept it, that you should follow the sensible course and band together for your own protection and welfare."

After Day had finished, a recess was called to take applications for union membership. The response was good and Local 574's strength climbed to over 3,000, as compared to about seventy-five members a year earlier. When the meeting reconvened, Carl Skoglund led off with an explanation of the next steps to be taken. The assembled workers then voted to strike if the bosses refused to meet the union's demands; a broad strike committee was elected; and the deadline for a strike was referred to the committee.

Parallel to the union campaign the Citizens Alliance had been shaping its own battle plan. On the heels of the coal strike a propagnada drive was launched to downgrade the significance of the union victory. It was stressed that no direct contract had been signed, or ordered by the Regional Labor Board, between the coal dealers and Local 574. According

to the coal bosses' story, they had simply filed a "voluntary"
statement of uniform wage scales with the Labor Board. When
the union had demanded a direct contract at a Labor Board
hearing, a spokesman for the coal employers had flatly refused the demand on the ground that "we have a deep-lying
principle involved." In line with that "principle" all trucking
bosses were being urged to concentrate on making individual
agreements with their employees.

Then during March the union got wind of an organizing
rally scheduled by the Citizens Alliance. Being an unknown
figure, I was assigned to cover the affair, posing as a cockroach boss. The main theme of the meeting was the "communist plot" to take over the city by imposing union control
over all businesses. All employers were urged to rally around
the Citizens Alliance to save the town from the union threat.
It was announced that steps were being taken to assure cooperation from the mayor and the police. Three classes of membership in the Citizens Alliance were offered to prospective recruits according to the service to be rendered. None of this
information came as a surprise to the union leadership, but
it was useful to know what was going on.

When the union demands were presented to the bosses after
the Shubert membership meeting, a sparring match developed.
Committees from the two sides met at the Labor Board's offices. The employers stated that they had come to the sessions
only as "a courtesy to the Labor Board." They concentrated
on requests for evidence that the union represented their employees. The union spokesmen countered by asking who the
employers' committee represented and what they proposed to
do about the union demands. The meeting ended on dead
center. Then on May 7 the employers addressed a letter to
the Labor Board focusing on the union recognition clause
in Local 574's demands. The letter stated that "the demand
for such closed union shop agreement is hereby definitely rejected."

On May 11 the Citizens Alliance issued a special bulletin
to its members warning of an imminent truck drivers' strike
intended to tie up all transportation in the city, including gasoline filling stations. It reported that an "Advisory Committee"
for employers was establishing a headquarters at the West
Hotel. Employers were urged to call this headquarters for
information and to report any developments they learned
about. "The principal issue involved in this strike is now

clearly and definitely brought out into the open," the bulletin asserted. "Officers of the General Drivers Union have frankly stated through the press that their main objective is unionization of every truck driver in Minneapolis and closed shop union control of all primary transportation." UNION RECOGNITION

As in the coal situation, union recognition was pinpointed AS as the key issue, and a victory for Local 574 was vital for PRIMARY all unions in the city if the open-shop rule of the Citizens Al-GOAL liance was to be smashed. When Hall reported the developments to Tobin, however, an indifferent reply was received to the effect that the union should proceed to negotiate through the Labor Board. It should be added that matters were not helped by Hall's continued practice of holding back per capita tax on new members, when Tobin knew that the local was experiencing some kind of growth.

In any case it was clear that we were heading toward what could become serious trouble with Tobin, who was basically opposed to what we were doing. When it came we would at least have seasoned troops capable of standing up against him. In the meantime some protective steps could be taken by involving the local AFL officialdom in our fight. The latter step was accomplished by getting the Central Labor Union on record in support of Local 574's demands. This implied that all AFL officials were taking some responsibility for the pending strike and were, therefore, obligated to support it.

Fears were voiced among the old-line labor skates that a general walkout in the trucking industry would be jeopardized by the unemployed taking the strikers' jobs. Their apprehension stemmed from the magnitude of the unemployed rolls. At that time some 30,000 workers were jobless in Minneapolis. Together with their families they comprised almost a third of the city's population. These thousands of social outcasts, within a city of less than half a million, were trying to subsist on a stingy government dole. The impossibility of their situation was making them fighting mad. Their mood was reflected in a protest demonstration on April 6, 1934, against the federal "work relief" program which was being operated on a pauper basis. Over 10,000 unemployed marched on City Hall in the protest. When they got there the police assaulted them with tear gas and clubs but the demonstrators stood their ground. In the hand-to-hand fighting that followed seven workers were injured — and eight cops.

As the Communist League saw it, these unemployed mil-

itants could be made allies of the union rather than a danger
to it. To accomplish this aim something more than rhetoric
was needed. It was necessary to give them a direct role in
the union walkout and to show that the alliance would not
be a one-sided affair. This was accomplished through the medium of Communist League members who had long been
active in the unemployed movement. Word was spread that
Local 574's strategy included the organization of an unemployed section of the union once it had been consolidated. In
addition, the union made preliminary arrangements to fight
for public relief for needy members as a safeguard against
the strikers being starved out. This put direct union weight
on the side of the unemployed and helped to cement the desired alliance. Leaders of the unemployed were consulted in
shaping the union's plans for picketing, an act that gave assurance they were not to be treated like country cousins.

Since picketing in an extensive truck strike would amount
to a virtual dragnet on the city's streets, problems that could
arise with farmers had to be considered. Farm trucks came
to the city hauling such things as fruit and vegetables to the
produce market, raw milk to creameries, and livestock to the
meat-packing plants. In general the union had no reason to
interfere with them, but at the outset of a large-scale trucking tie-up some of the farmers would most likely run into
difficulties that might antagonize them. A way had to be found
to quickly solve any problems that arose and for that purpose advance consultation with the farmers was needed.

Here again the Communist League was able to make the
necessary connections. It had contacts within the Minnesota
Farmers' Holiday Association, a militant organization that
had acted to prevent foreclosure sale of farms, conducted milk
strikes for higher prices from creameries, and in general was
hostile to the city-based capitalist overlords. Close working
relations were established with John Bosch, president of the
association, who assured the union of full cooperation in the
pending strike.

Another step in preparation for the walkout was initiated
by Carl Skoglund, who proposed to the organizing committee that a womens' auxiliary be formed. The aim would be
to draw in wives, girl friends, sisters, and mothers of union
members. Instead of having their morale corroded by financial
difficulties they would face during the strike, he pointed out,
they should be drawn into the thick of battle where they could

learn unionism through firsthand participation. His plan was approved by the committee, and I was assigned to present it at a union membership meeting. The proposal was adopted, although not with much enthusiasm. Afterward I got some needling, especially from men who saw in their union activity a way to get an occasional night out, but all this stopped suddenly when the women went into action later on.

Launching of the auxiliary project was undertaken by Marvel Scholl, who was married to me, and Clara Dunne, Grant's wife. They began by speaking at meetings of various sections of the union where demands upon the bosses were being drawn up. At first they were received with an air of courteous toleration. Then some men began to ask questions about the project, wanting to know what the women could do in a strike. Clara and Marvel explained that staffing a union commissary, handling telephones, helping in a first-aid station, were only a few of the many things women could find to do during the fight. After a time the men began to talk to their wives about it, and to the surprise of some, they found the women were interested. Before long a number of the women telephoned Marvel and Clara, asking for more details about the proposed auxiliary. They also volunteered information about special skills they had as cooks, waitresses, nurses, or office workers.

This development coincided with other preparations for the strike. A big garage building at 1900 Chicago Avenue was rented to serve as an operational headquarters. Besides its capacity to handle picket mobilizations, the building was large enough for a commissary, the necessary offices, and a mechanical repair department. It was also to house a field hospital which was being organized with the help of Dr. H. P. McCrimmon, whose services had been acquired by the union. This step alone showed that the union was determined to fight and that it would take care of its wounded. A garage had been rented because the strike would be a mobile one, with expanded use of the cruising picket squads which had been developed during the coal strike. In that department, charts of the city were being made up, picketing instructions drafted, and picket captains selected. On the whole the union was pretty much ready for action.

The careful organizational spadework had a salutary effect on the workers as was shown when the union called a meeting at Eagles Hall on the evening of May 15, 1934. The mem-

bership turnout was massive; many women were present from
the auxiliary; and in general a confident fighting mood prevailed. Although she was probably as scared as I had been
at the Shubert Theater, Marvel Scholl got up before the meeting and pledged the auxiliary's support to Local 574. The
negotiating committee reported the insolent refusal of the bosses
to deal with the union and Bill Brown made a stem-winding
speech sounding the call to battle. When a motion was made
to go on strike the membership gave unanimous approval
in a standing vote, not entirely in keeping with Tobin's pre-
scripts. The meeting then adjourned to 1900 Chicago Avenue
where women and men alike joined in putting the finishing
touches on preparation for the walkout.

Organizing the Strike

Local 574's combat leaders, acting through the organizing committee, had no illusions about the gravity of the impending conflict. They were fully aware that the bosses would try to smash the strike. If the union was to win, a tremendous battle would be necessary. Under the pressures of such a fierce struggle, maneuvers detrimental to the union could be expected from the Labor Board and from Governor Olson. We could also anticipate weakness on the part of the city's AFL officialdom, which was bound to be squeamish about physical combat and prone to urge the workers to rely completely on Olson. In the last analysis the outcome of the strike would hinge on the fighting capacity of the union ranks.

Seeking to impart this understanding to the membership, the combat leaders prepared to teach the workers the ins and outs of fighting for their rights. This circumstance made the strike quite exceptional. Fighting spirit in the ranks was usually restrained and dampened by the AFL officials, while in this case a militant struggle was being organized by what had become the key section of the top union leadership.

Seldom anywhere, in fact, had there been such a well-prepared strike. When the sun rose on May 16, 1934, the headquarters at 1900 Chicago Avenue was a beehive of activity. Union carpenters and plumbers were installing gas stoves, sinks, and serving counters in the commissary. The Cooks and Waiters Union sent experts on mass cooking and serving to help organize things and train the volunteer help. Working in two twelve-hour shifts, over 100 volunteers served 4,000 to 5,000 people daily. Sandwiches and coffee were always available and a hot meal was served whenever the commissary's resources and the circumstances of the strike permitted. In addition, arrangements were made so that key personnel could sleep in or near the headquarters for the duration.

Committees were set up to promote material aid. They solicited friendly grocers for staples to be used in the commissary and to help out the needy families of strikers. Similar donations were also received from sympathetic farmers. The committees fought city hall to get public relief for union members and the facts of life were explained to landlords who pressed the workers for rent payments. Money donations from other unions helped to stock the commissary, as well as to buy gasoline for the cruising picket squads and medical supplies for the union's emergency hospital. Even Governor Olson contributed $500 to Local 574.

The union's medical staff included Dr. McCrimmon and two interns from the University of Minnesota hospital who volunteered their services during their off hours. Three trained nurses headed up a larger volunteer staff that provided such efficient care that, despite the many open wounds treated, not one bad infection developed. The hospital was supervised by Mrs. Vera McCormack, a skilled technician whom everyone fondly called "Mac." To avoid air pollution in the hospital and commissary, picket cars were pushed into and out of the headquarters.

About a score of skilled auto mechanics had turned to, bringing their tools with them, to keep the strikers' cars in working order. The former tool crib and supply room in the big garage was turned into a general office where volunteers did the typing and mimeographing and signed up new members pouring into the union. An organized guard was maintained in and around the headquarters to watch for police intrusions, prevent drinking, cool down temper flareups, and keep order. Except at critical times, when everyone worked to the point of exhaustion, the various assignments were rotated.

Special attention was given to keeping the workers informed about the strike's progress and helping them to answer lies peddled by the bosses. Each evening a general assembly was held at the headquarters for this purpose. Reports were made by the strike leaders, guest speakers were invited from other unions to help morale through expressions of solidarity, and some form of entertainment usually followed. A loudspeaker system was installed so that packed meetings could hear what was said, as could the overflow crowds outside, which often numbered two to three thousand.

There were also regular meetings of the strike committee of seventy-five, which had been elected by the union membership. This body, which made the general decisions about strike policy, had in turn designated a small subcommittee to handle complaints. Most of the complaints had to do with requests from cockroach bosses who asked for special permission to operate their trucks. Usually the requests were unjustified and were automatically turned down, but having a special committee to handle these matters saved unnecessary wear and tear on the picket commanders.

Another subcommittee was charged with the responsibility of arranging legal assistance for pickets arrested during the strike. The first lawyer obtained proved to be a shyster whose method was to make a deal with the public prosecutor. In return for dismissal of cases against a few pickets he would plead a larger number guilty. He did that just once and the union fired him. We didn't expect our lawyer to win every case, but at least we wanted him to fight for us. The union committee went in search of one who would.

Picket dispatching was assigned to Ray Dunne and me. This was Ray's first official function in Local 574, although he had headed the Communist League fraction in the union from the start of the organizing drive in coal. Previously he had been handicapped by loss of his coal job which stripped him of a formal basis for union membership. Now, however, he was able to step forward as a volunteer supporter of the strike, along with hundreds of other individual workers. Many in the strike committee were aware of his impressive trade-union credentials, and he was given an important assignment accordingly.

Working beside Ray, as had been the case earlier with Carl Skoglund, impressed upon me the experience and education one gains through membership in a revolutionary socialist party. He knew a lot about conducting a strike, and like Carl, he taught me a lot about the team concept in leadership. Ray was a superb combat leader with a clear sense of purpose, backed up by strong willpower and the ability to keep a cool head in critical situations. He not only taught by the example he set, never shirking either hazardous or minor tasks; he also gave others leeway for initiative, seeking only to safeguard against serious blunders. His criticisms were presented constructively with the aim of helping others to learn. Never a dabbler at anything he did, Ray tried to find some role for everyone who wanted to help. "Don't write people off lightly," he often said. "It's not the mark of an organizer."

As dispatchers, Ray and I were in charge of all picketing

assignments and it was our responsibility to direct tactical operations. We had a special staff at our disposal to handle the telephones and operate a shortwave radio used to monitor police calls. Teenage volunteers with motorcycles were organized into an efficient courier service. Scooting around the city under strict orders to stay out of the fighting, they served as the eyes and ears of the picket dispatchers and as a swift means of contact with picket captains. So many cars and individually owned trucks were volunteered that we had more than enough to achieve the high degree of mobility required in the strike. Trucks were used to transport stationary picket details and their relief shifts to truck terminals, the market area, wholesale houses, and other places where trucks normally operated. Picket crews also kept a vigil at points where the main highways crossed the city limits.

Cruising squads in autos were assigned, district by district, to sweep through the streets on the lookout for scab trucking operations. A captain was designated for each of these squads and for each detachment of stationary pickets. At all times a reserve force with the necessary transportation was kept on hand at the strike headquarters. In situations where large forces were involved, a field commander was appointed and a command post set up to coordinate activities and keep in touch with the headquarters. Special cruising squads with handpicked crews were constantly at the disposal of the picket dispatchers. They were captained by qualified leaders who carried credentials authorizing them to supersede all other authority in the field. These squads were used for special assignments on their own, and they were sent into tense situations to marshal the union forces and lead the fight.

Assembling the mass forces for such extensive picketing proved to be no problem at all. As soon as the strike was called, new members poured into Local 574 from all sections of the trucking industry. In no time at all the union almost doubled its mid-April strength, reaching a figure of nearly 6,000. The union's approach to the unemployed workers brought spectacular results. Hundreds upon hundreds of jobless poured into the strike headquarters, volunteering their services; and they fought like tigers in the battles that followed. Unorganized workers from other industries came forward. Together with women and men from other unions, they came to the strike headquarters at the end of their day's work, ready to help in whatever way they could. Deep in the night they would finally stretch out wherever they found a place to get a little sleep before returning to their jobs. A significant number of college students pitched in to help the union. All in all, pickets were on hand by the thousands.

A majority of the city's population proved sympathetic to the strike and soon a spontaneous intelligence service was in operation. People telephoned reports of scab activities, and other information was mailed in anonymously, often with the postage having been paid by some unknowing employer. Typists, even personal secretaries, slipped in an extra carbon to make a copy for the union when a boss dictated something they felt the strikers should know about. Material arrived that had obviously been salvaged from wastebaskets, some of it coming from the offices of the Citizens Alliance itself.

As matters now stood, the union had its strategy worked out, the necessary forces had been mobilized and picketing operations were planned with military precision. The next step was to begin the big push against the employers. Trucking operations had to remain tied up, despite all attempts to use scabs working under police protection, until the employers agreed to deal with the union. At the outset the coal heavers were about the only ones who had experience in Local 574's picketing techniques — in fact, many of the pickets had little or no previous experience at all. Whenever they found a truck on the streets they escorted it to the strike headquarters. Soon the area around 1900 Chicago Avenue was crowded with a motley assemblage of vehicles loaded with milk, coal, tobacco, tea and coffee, hogs, cattle, and diverse other things, including a few loads of hay.

Policy briefings of the green pickets soon corrected this and thereafter when doubt arose about what to do in a given situation they communicated with headquarters instead of bringing the rig in. Farmers caught in the dragnet were especially indignant, but with the help of the Farmers' Holiday Association the union worked out a policy agreeable to them, except in the case of the market gardeners with whom we were to have some difficulties. For a couple of days there was trouble with a few filling stations that tried to operate. They attempted to play a cat-and-mouse game with pickets, closing down and then reopening, until the special cruising squads stepped in and definitively settled the matter.

While all this was going on, talk about joining Local 574 spread rapidly among fleet drivers at the Yellow Cab Company.

When the employer got wind of it he tried to set up a company union and the drivers reacted angrily. On the second day of Local 574's walkout they sent a delegation to the strike committee asking that they be allowed to take a hand in the fight being waged by the truck drivers and other workers. Despite the existance of a miniscule local union of individual cab owners and their relief drivers, the strike committee agreed to sign up the Yellow Cab drivers. Cruising squads were sent out to notify all taxi drivers of a meeting at strike headquarters that night. Upon coming together they voted to go on strike, and within hours not a cab was to be found in operation.

As this episode graphically demonstrated, Local 574 had become a power to be reckoned with. Its effective picketing activities had become stabilized. Nothing moved on wheels without the union's permission.

Warfare Begins

The scope and power of the strike had taken the trucking bosses and the Citizens Alliance leaders completely by surprise. While figuring out what to do, they had simply kept their trucks off the streets and the union had held sway with little opposition. Now, however, the workers were about to get a taste of the measures the capitalists resort to in a showdown— repressive force and violence.

The capitalist press stepped up its attacks on the union, twisting and distorting the facts about the strike. Proclaiming their intention to "keep the streets open," the bosses recruited scab drivers and thugs. At the command of the Citizens Alliance, the cops jumped into action against the union. The court records showed only eighteen arrests during the first two days of the strike; on the third and fourth days, by contrast, 151 pickets were hauled into court. Fines of as much as fifty dollars were levied against them and seventeen got workhouse sentences of from ten to forty-five days. On Friday, May 18, 1934, a "citizens rally" of the employing class was held at which a "law and order" committee was chosen. As reported in a Citizens Alliance bulletin obtained by the union, the committee was set up to organize special deputies, acting in consultation with the sheriff and police chief. A special headquarters for the deputies was rented at 1328 Hennepin Avenue and equipped with a commissary and hospital, emulating the arrangements at the union's strike headquarters.

In their first attempt to break the picket lines, the Citizens Alliance strategists resorted to a flank attack, using a peculiarity about the city market which had not received sufficient attention from the union. Small truck farmers rented stalls in the market area where they put their produce on display and corner grocers came to buy it from them. Since chain stores were not yet crowding out the little grocers, trade of this kind was quite brisk. These farmers belonged to the Market Gardeners Association which had no connection with the Farmers' Holiday movement. The union had made no direct arrangement with them and, as a result, they were unintentionally hurt by the strike. Aware that the truck gardeners were quite upset about it, the Citizens Alliance strategists sought to use them as a front for a strikebreaking attack on the union.

Reports were published in the capitalist press that the "market gardeners have organized against the strike." A convoy of farmers' trucks was started toward the market, escorted by about seventy sheriff's deputies. They were soon intercepted by cruising picket squads and an hour-long running battle followed along the route toward the market. Caught in the middle of a fight between the pickets and deputies, most of the farmers turned around and went home; only three trucks got through to the market.

After this experience the union assured the Market Gardeners Association safe-conduct to peddle their produce directly to small grocers throughout the town. In this roundabout way they could do business without injuring the strike and the union could keep the market closed without hurting them. The truck farmers accepted the proposal and became neutral, some even friendly, toward the strike.

Having failed in their attempt to use the farmers against the strike, the bosses came out in the open in their attack on the union. Scabs were used on the morning of Saturday, May 19, to load two trucks at the Bearman Fruit Company in the market under the protection of a big gang of cops and hired thugs wielding clubs and blackjacks. Union cruising squads were sent to reinforce the picket line and in the ensuing battle the barehanded strikers used whatever means they could hastily find to defend themselves. A number of the pickets were badly injured, as were a few of the cops and thugs. A written account of the fight was later given to me by one of the picket captains, Jack Maloney. (He is listed in the strike records as Severson, his stepfather's name, which he used for a time.)

Jack wrote in part: ". . . we had quite a beef, several of us were clubbed by the police. I, for one, was dragged into Bearman's unconscious. When I came to, Harold Beal and Louie Scullard were also in custody inside there and the patrol wagon came shortly. I was bleeding quite heavily from the head and after Harold and Louie were put in the wagon, the cops took me out and when they let go of me at the wagon I fell down. In the ensuing melee the pickets picked me up and carried me over toward Sixth and Hennepin. They called an ambulance and I was taken to the General Hospital, as were some of the other pickets. After the doctors had patched up my head I was placed in a room, waiting to go to jail. The business agent of the steamfitters union came to where I was sitting and said to the woman at the desk, 'I will take this man.' We walked out into the hallway and he said, 'Get the hell out of here quick.'"

Jack's experience shows how hospitals are used against strikers. When an injured picket is brought in they notify the police and cooperate in holding the victim for arrest. That is one reason why the union had its own hospital at strike headquarters. Whenever possible our wounded were brought there for medical care. They were taken to regular hospitals only when necessary for treatment of serious injuries. By the time Saturday's events were over, every picket understood the need for this policy and thereafter it was scrupulously followed.

In the evening of that day a deadly trap was sprung on the union. It had been set in what was called Newspaper Alley at the loading docks of the two main dailies which were housed in neighboring buildings. Reports began to reach strike headquarters about preparations to deliver bundles of newspapers under strong police protection. As picket dispatchers, Ray and I were feeling out the situation, not wanting a repetition of the morning's experience at Bearman Fruit. Then an agent provocateur got on the loudspeaker and asked for two or three truckloads of pickets, calling for women to pile into the trucks with the men. Up to then he had worked hard and loyally in the strike, ingratiating himself to a point where he was fully trusted. Pretending to be relaying orders from the dispatchers he sent the pickets to Newspaper Alley. It was an ambush in which they were beaten viciously by police clubs and by saps in the hands of the hired thugs.

Soon the picket trucks were back, carrying bleeding victims who were rushed into the hospital at strike headquarters. Some with broken bones, five of them women, had to be sent to a regular hospital for more complete care. A search of the provocateur and his car produced membership cards in various unions and Farmer-Labor Party clubs along with a Burns

Detective Agency badge and credentials. As word of the vicious attack got around sympathetic druggists donated medical supplies to the union. Shocked doctors and nurses in the regular hospitals began to help spirit pickets away after they had been treated so that the cops couldn't grab them.

Shortly after the Newspaper Alley victims had been brought in, two city police barged into the strike headquarters claiming that the pickets had kidnapped a scab driver. If he wasn't handed over, they threatened, the strike leaders would be arrested and, clubs at the ready, they started for the picket dispatcher's office. All the pentup wrath against police brutality was vented on them. Within minutes they lay unconscious in front of the headquarters where they stayed until an ambulance came for them in response to a call put in by the union. So many pickets had gone for the two police that they got in one another's way. Sherman Oakes, a coal and ice driver, swung a club at one cop and accidentally hit another striker, Bill Abar, breaking his arm. Sherman burst into tears. We couldn't figure out whether it was because he hit Bill or because he missed the cop.

In its Saturday evening edition, the Minneapolis Journal said, "Fierce rioting broke out Saturday as 425 special officers went into action to break the Truck Drivers strike." A common trick of the capitalist press is illustrated here. With a simple wiggle of the editor's pencil, criminal police assaults on peaceful pickets are transformed into "fierce rioting" by the victims. Also to be noted is the flat statement of the intention "to break the Truck Drivers strike."

The Sunday morning papers dealt with the strike in a similar vein, claiming that hundreds were volunteering as special police. All day long, late into the evening, radio broadcasts continued the scare campaign started by the newspapers. By the day's end, over 2,000 deputies were reported mobilized. In reality, according to official records obtained later by the union, only 544 deputies were enrolled as of Monday, mainly among such types as businessmen, professional people, and salesmen, with a few workers being suckered in. These facts, of course, did not deter the authors of the published reports, which were deliberately exaggerated in order to throw fright into the strikers by making them believe that the whole town was mobilizing against them.

Contrary to the bosses' hopes and expectations, the strikers were not exactly paralyzed with fear at the prospect of facing an army of cops and deputies. Instead they began to show the positive side of the workers' illusions about capitalist democracy.

The negative side of their beliefs lies in the assumption that they have inviolable democratic rights under capitalist rule. It is a mistaken assumption that can remain intact, in the long run, only until they try to exercise such rights in the class struggle. When that happens the workers learn that they have been the victims of an illusion. Yet they still feel entitled to the rights involved and they will fight all the harder to make them a reality. A negative misconception then becomes transformed into a positive aspiration, as was about to happen in Minneapolis.

Up to now the workers had gone about their activities barehanded; but they found that attempts to exercise their right to peacefully picket were being repressed with police clubs and blackjacks. They decided to take steps to enforce their democratic right to prevent scabs from grabbing their jobs. It would have been a tactical blunder for members of an isolated vanguard to attempt measures such as the strikers were about to take; they would only get themselves clobbered by the police. In this case, however, the means used in self-defense had their origin in a spontaneous mass mood that had been generated by capitalist repression. Since these means were appropriately limited in the given situation to matching the police club for club, the tactics employed were completely valid.

All day Sunday the strikers equipped themselves for battle. Baseball bats appeared; garden hoses were cut into short lengths, lead washers were tamped into the hollow and the ends closed with friction tape to make an improvised sap. Volunteers from the Carpenters' Union sawed two-by-twos into club lengths. A sympathizer came to the strike headquarters pulling a child's coaster wagon loaded with bannister posts taken from the stairway at home, his wife steadying the load. To make improvised helmets, heavy cardboard was stuffed inside the sweatband of hats. A fellow striker would be asked to test it out with a club, and if the result was negative, more cardboard would be added.

In the fighting that was to follow a division of labor was made; men did the picketing where combat was involved while the women helped the strike in a whole series of ways. Most of the headquarters functions were taken over by women. They picketed the newspaper buildings to denounce the boss press

for its lies about the strike; protest actions were conducted by
them at City Hall; and they went to other unions soliciting
support. Before long, delegation after delegation from other
unions began appearing at the strike headquarters asking
what they could do to help. In his account mentioned before,
Jack Maloney gave a description that reflects the general mood
in Local 574's army.

He wrote: "In my opinion the weekend activity at 1900 Chicago was prompted not only in anticipation of what was ahead
but actually by what had [occurred]. It was not just specu-
lation and leadership counseling that spurred the activity but
actual events, in my way of looking at things. This is a very
important factor because, to me at least (and I was very
young, twenty-two), the employers were ready and determined
to kill if needed to maintain their control. I was determined to
make them prove it and so it was with so many men at that
time. They knew what to expect on Monday or the next day
and they were ready to 'go for broke.' At Bearman's the pickets had a sample of what to expect. The cops won that battle
but on Monday the pickets gave their receipt for Saturday."

In the Monday confrontation, to which Jack referred, two
organized and disciplined forces were to face each other, club
against club, in a battle fought along military lines. We didn't
know how many different attempts the bosses would make
to begin moving trucks on Monday, but a major effort could
be expected in the market district. Perishable foods were handled
there, and this gave the Citizens Alliance propaganda cover
for a strikebreaking attack. In fact, the union was receiving tips
from friendly sources about plans to open the market houses
on Monday. Since, from the union's viewpoint, the market
was a good battleground, we were not disturbed by the news.
We simply concentrated on preparations for a fight there.

A "coffee-and" station for cruising pickets had been set up
in the AFL building at 614 First Avenue North, right at the
edge of the market district. An unusual coming and going
of pickets at this place began early Sunday evening. On the
surface it seemed to reflect increased cruising squad activity
but of each carload of five or six who entered the building
only two or three came back out. In this surreptitious manner about 600 men had been concentrated in the AFL hall
before morning, all armed with clubs.

Around four A. M. Monday small picket lines appeared
in front of the market houses. Larger numbers of pickets, their

union buttons temporarily concealed, fanned out in strategic positions around the district. An example of their ingenuity was shown by Steve Glaser, a short, stocky warehouseman who walked on a stiff leg. He looked quite harmless before the fight started. Then he jerked a big club out of his pants leg and moved around with great agility. In addition to these forces a reserve of some 900 was kept at the strike headquarters, ready to move at a moment's notice. All in all, the union had a strong army deployed for battle and it had been done in a way that would give the cops some surprises.

Several hundred uniformed cops were on hand in the market, along with comparable numbers of special deputies. The cops were on the prod, feeling cocky after their Saturday exploits. Among the deputies was a wealthy playboy garbed in a polo hat. Like the rest of his ilk, he anticipated having a bit of a lark as he went about the business of clubbing down working-class sheep. About nine A. M. scab drivers backed six trucks up to the loading dock at the Gamble Robinson Company on Fifth Street. Large numbers of pickets quickly gathered there and, as a loaded truck started to move out, a cop slugged a striker. The union men charged in and the fight was on.

With the cops deployed on the assumption that they knew the union's strength, the 600 pickets waiting at the AFL hall were ordered into battle and they moved out in military formation. Fighting soon spread to three or four other market houses where preparations were being made to open for business. Cops and deputies alike were falling, amid cheers from among the many bystanders, some of whom pitched in to help the strikers. With the workers challenging them, club against club, most of the deputies took to their heels, leaving the uniformed cops on their own. More police were rushed in from posts in the main business district. The union quickly countered this move by summoning hundreds of reserves from the strike headquarters.

In an act of desperation, the cops drew their guns, threatening to shoot; but they seemed hesitant to resort to such extreme measures, and that gave us a little time to do something about it. As matters stood they were pretty well bunched up, with an open field of fire against the strikers. To solve the problem they had to be scattered among the pickets. The remaining reserves at strike headquarters were loaded into trucks, the lead truck driven by Bob Bell, a huge man and

Above and below: scenes of heavy fighting between pickets and police reinforced by deputies in city marketplace during May strike.

utterly fearless. He was told to rush to the market, ignoring
all traffic rules, and to drive right into the midst of the cops.
Bob did just that. The pickets jumped out of the truck onto
the cops who, being unable to shoot without hitting one another, had to continue fighting with clubs. After that, Police
Chief Johannes decided to call it a day.

No less than thirty uniformed cops and a number of deputies had to be hospitalized. Union wounded were taken to
strike headquarters where all were taken care of, except for
a few with broken bones who needed regular hospital treatment. The strangest wound on our side was received by Harold Beal, who was virtually scalped by a glancing blow from
a club. Despite our casualties we were in a favorable position.
In a three-hour slugfest the union had fought the trained police to a draw, and not a single truck had been moved.

As warfare raged in the market, 700 members of the wom-
en's auxiliary, led by Marvel Scholl and Clara Dunne, marched
on city hall. Crowds gathered on the sidewalks to watch them
pass with their Local 574 banner at the head of the column
and many onlookers joined the procession. When they got
to city hall their way was barred by nervous cops with guns.
Finally, a small delegation was allowed to go in to present
their demands upon Mayor Bainbridge. Meanwhile the rest
of the women carried on a protest demonstration outside the
building. Bainbridge refused to see the delegation but the evening papers reported their demands: that the mayor fire Chief
Johannes, withdraw all deputies, and stop interfering with the
pickets.

Trade unionists throughout the city were enraged about the
police brutality and they were stimulated by Local 574's heroic
fight. This led to a highly unusual course of action in the
building trades. Demands to call a strike arose in the ranks,
this time not in their narrow craft interests, but in solidarity
with the embattled truck drivers. The pressure became so great
that officials of the Building Trades Council recommended
a sympathy strike. Craft by craft, the building-trades unions
voted to call a holiday for the duration of the drivers' walkout. One of these unions, the Electrical Workers, marched in
a body to 1900 Chicago Avenue and put themselves at the
disposal of Local 574's strike committee. This action had
been inspired by two members of the union, Oscar Coover,
Sr., and Chester Johnson, both of whom also belonged to
the Communist League. Although sympathy strikes were more

or less limited to the building trades, financial and moral support for Local 574 was voted by the executive board of the AFL Central Labor Union.

Early Monday afternoon Police Chief Johannes ordered the whole police force on twenty-four-hour duty, and he asked the American Legion to provide 1,500 deputies. Strikers found on the streets wearing bandages were picked up by the cops. The "Citizens Committee for Law and Order," operating from the Radisson Hotel, rushed a request to businessmen for help in recruiting deputies "personally known to you for their integrity." The written request stated: "Every citizen of this type possible must be deputized either as a special police officer or deputy sheriff. Report and have others report, with credentials from you, if possible, to headquarters at 1328 Hennepin Avenue, in rough clothes and ready for service." Having been frustrated in its first major strikebreaking attempt, the Citizens Alliance was desperately looking for more police muscle, still confident that the union could be beaten into submission.

Tuesday morning the market district was filled with people. Spectators came by the thousands, packing the sidewalks and peering from the windows and roofs of buildings, hoping to see a repetition of Monday's fighting. A local radio station, KSTP, had portable equipment on the scene with an announcer ready to broadcast a blow-by-blow account of the day's happenings.

Local 574 was there in force, supported by many volunteer pickets from other unions. During the night the battleground had been studied to determine the best strategic placement of the union forces. Little more than that could be done, however, concerning overall guidance of the fighting because of the huge numbers of people present. The union cause would have to rest entirely on the readiness of the strikers to give battle and the ability of their picket captains to lead them. There proved to be no cause for concern on either count.

Most of the city's uniformed cops were present as well as several hundred deputies. Some of the deputies had gotten a bellyful Monday and failed to show up again, but these were replaced by new ones who had been recruited overnight. Since the deputies had run away the day before, uniformed cops had now been put in charge of each contingent in an effort to make them stand and fight. All told, the repressive force numbered over 1,500.

The morning paper had announced that the produce houses were going to move perishables, and a few scabs surrounded by cops, started to load a truck. Unlike Monday's events, however, they didn't get to the point of trying to move the rig. Tension was so thick that one could almost touch it in the air and anything could trigger the pending battle. Suddenly a sound of shattering glass was heard, as someone threw a produce crate through a window, and before the echo died away a free-for-all had started.

The pickets charged the deputies first and soon noticed that many uniformed cops were tending to hang back. Obviously these cops resented being deserted by the deputies Monday and they didn't seem to relish another clubbing match. Sensing this mood among some of the cops, the pickets continued to concentrate mainly on the deputies. Soon even the bystanders were getting in licks in support of the strikers. Finding themselves mousetrapped, many deputies dropped their clubs and ripped off their badges, trying with little success to seek anonymity in the hostile crowd. By this time the pickets were also zeroing in on uniformed cops who had gotten into the thick of the fight. The scene of battle spread as cops and deputies alike were driven from the market. The deputies were chased clear back to their headquarters, the strikers mopping up on stragglers along the way.

In less than an hour after the battle started there wasn't a cop to be seen in the market, and pickets were directing traffic in the now peaceful district. For good measure all police were run out of the vicinity of the strike headquarters and they were kept away for the duration of the walkout. Injuries in the fighting were heavy on both sides and two special deputies were killed: Peter Erath and C. Arthur Lyman, the latter a member of the board of directors of the Citizens Alliance.

While the struggle was going on in the market, a telegram came from Tobin, ordering the union to seek arbitration of the dispute. At the time the strike leaders were quite busy and the telegram lay on the dispatchers' table at headquarters. Francis H. Shoemaker, a sympathetic U. S. congressman, was snooping around and he came upon the message. Shoemaker, who had already proven to be irresponsible, adventuristic, and an exhibitionist to boot, took it upon himself to send Tobin an answer. It said: "Keep your scabby nose and scaly face out. This is a fight for human rights. Your rat job not involved."

The big catch was that he signed Bill Brown's name to the reply, making it appear to be an official union response. We had trouble enough on our hands without going out of the way to antagonize Tobin. So Shoemaker's message was officially repudiated and the strike headquarters was declared off limits to him. Tobin appeared to accept the explanation, since he attacked Shoemaker editorially in the next issue of the *Teamsters Journal,* but the episode nevertheless added to his mounting grudge against Local 574.

Considerable nervousness had developed in the upper echelons of the local AFL officialdom about the course the strike was taking. So they decided to make a bid for a truce in the fighting and try to bring the situation under Governor Olson's control. Toward noon on Tuesday a joint committee from the Central Labor Union, Building Trades Council and Teamsters Joint Council called on Chief Johannes, asking him to call off the cops and stop trying to move trucks. He took the committee to see Sheriff Wall, and there it was agreed to call in the governor. Olson soon arrived, bringing along General E. A. Walsh, Commander of the National Guard. Representatives of Local 574 and the trucking employers were then brought into the discussion. Speaking for Local 574 were Bill Brown, Grant Dunne, and Ed Hedlund; for the bosses there were W. M. Hardin, M. A. Lehman, and G. F. Williams.

The meeting was told that the Labor Board was readying a proposal for settlement of the strike, and after some argument a twenty-four-hour truce was agreed upon. It provided for suspension of truck traffic and the complete closing of the market place. In return, Local 574 agreed to suspend picketing except for observers to see that the truce was carried out. The representatives of the employers and Local 574 signed the truce, as did Walter Frank of the Lathers, and Joel Anderson of the Steamfitters on behalf of the building-trades unions, which had declared a sympathy strike.

Before the truce period had ended Johannes announced that trucks would be moved under police protection and Local 574 quickly responded with a statement that picketing would be resumed. Mayor Bainbridge then called on Olson to mobilize the guard and the governor promptly did so, asking at the same time for a twenty-four-hour extension of the truce. Local 574 denounced the calling up of the National Guard as an act of intimidation and demanded that it be demobilized. Olson was told that extension of the truce would be acceptable to the union only if there was a continued ban on all truck traffic by the struck firms. The governor decided to keep the troops off the streets, the initial terms of the truce were extended and a basis was established for some form of contract negotiations to begin.

Due to a regional peculiarity within a nation under firm capitalist rule, a local condition approximating dual power had temporarily arisen. The authorities could exercise control over the class struggle then raging only insofar as they proceeded in a manner acceptable to Local 574 and its allies. A combination of factors had brought about this situation. Being fearful about relying on Olson to get their strikebreaking done, the bosses had decided to depend on the local police apparatus, which was controlled by old-line capitalist politicians. However, the cops proved incapable of doing the dirty job so the mayor then tried to put Olson on the spot by demanding help from the National Guard.

This demand could not be met by the governor without raising a danger to him from another quarter. If he ordered the troops into naked strikebreaking action, it would jeopardize vital political support that he enjoyed from the labor movement. Olson was sharply reminded of the political threat from this quarter when Local 574 promptly denounced his action in calling up the Guard and demanded that it be demobilized. He decided to back away from any idea of using the troops and this kept things at a standoff in local class relations.

If a comparable situation had existed nationally, what began as a simple trade-union action could have broadened into a sweeping social conflict leading toward a revolutionary confrontation for state power. As matters stood, however, the conflict did not reach beyond the city limits. On that narrow scale nothing more could be accomplished than to fight to a finish in the battle for union recognition. Considering the existing conditions, a victory on that issue alone would be a matter of no small consequence. The oppressive open-shop rule of the Citizens Alliance would be definitively broken, and the way would be opened to make Minneapolis a union town.

This perspective was advanced to the workers at a massive labor rally held on Wednesday evening, May 23. It took place at the Parade Grounds, a big open field opposite an armory, which was available for public functions. Over 5,000 were on hand before the scheduled starting time and people kept coming by the hundreds. Many had quickly bolted an evening meal and hurried to the rally in their work clothes, some bringing their children with them. Those present included women and men, young and old, employed and jobless, organized and unorganized. Together they made up a cross-section of the working class. When the speaking program began a hush fell over the throng, people straining to hear what the strike leaders had to say.

"If we don't get full union recognition and an acceptable settlement," Bill Brown declared, "Local 574 will continue the strike and we will call upon all the workers to support us." The huge audience roared its approval.

Trickery in the Negotiations

When heavy fighting broke out in the market on Monday, May 21, 1934, Local 574's struggle in Minneapolis became headline news throughout the country. Wire services flashed reports of the conflict to all newspapers. Radio networks broadcast excerpts from KSTP's on-the-scene account of the routing of the uniformed cops and deputies on Tuesday. Newsreels, which were then a feature of motion picture entertainment, showed combat scenes filmed during the Tuesday battle. Workers everywhere reacted enthusiastically to the news. Audiences in movie houses broke out in cheers at the sight of pickets clubbing cops for a change, since in most strikes it was entirely the other way around. It did the workers good to see unionists standing their ground against the police and, in fact, giving more punishment than they received.

These reports gave the central leaders of the Communist League in New York their first inkling of the full scope of the Teamster strike. They were especially disturbed by news accounts of Governor Olson's mobilization of the National Guard which could become a serious threat to the union. A decision was quickly made to send Jim Cannon, the party's national secretary, to help the Teamster comrades. He made the trip to Minneapolis by plane, a quite expensive mode of travel in those days. This put a heavy strain on the meager budget of the small Communist League; but since it was the fastest way to go and speed was decisive, the means to buy a ticket were scraped up the hard way.

This action corresponded with the duty of the national leadership. When any section of a revolutionary party is involved in a critical action, the local comrades should not be left to their own resources. The national leadership must give them all possible assistance and, in the last analysis, take the responsibility for the party's role in the action.

Writing to me years later about this aspect of the situation,

Ray Dunne recalled: "We, that is the local party fraction, were as confident about the May outcome as we were about the coal strike. We had good reasons, because out of the coal yards we had recruited [into the union— FD] hundreds of mostly young, eager, battle-tested activists and organizers. They recruited and trained hundreds of other new drivers and inside workers. Most important, we recruited by the threes and tens for our party. . . . I'm quite sure— here looking backward— that we made a grievous mistake in our failure to keep the party center informed of the fast-developing situation in Minneapolis. This must be registered as a bad error in judgment. We talked about this, Carl [Skoglund] and I, but agreed that to do so would be loading onto New York local problems that would only add to troubles in the center with which they were confronted, due to an already developing faction fight with a petty-bourgeois grouping.

"This error was brought home to us when Jim made his trip *by air* to Minneapolis at the end of the May strike. His attitude and grasp of the local situation was something almost completely new and strange. [Here Ray appears to be contrasting his appreciation of Jim's visit to unhappy experiences in the past with top leaders of the Communist Party who had come to intervene in local situations— FD]. Being the Bolshevik he was, he grasped several things that reinforced the party and its role both locally and, still more important, nationwide . . . By reason of Jim's visit, [projection of a national] outlook for an escalation, for an organizational advance— which did not cross but fitted in with our local outlook — did, in fact, lift the whole struggle to a higher political and strategic plane."

The national outlook to which Ray referred had to do with the relationship of the Minneapolis strike to the political work of the Communist League as a whole. Up to then a lot of wiseacres had sneered at the Trotskyist movement and dismissed its role because it was small and weak. Now, Communist League members were leading a tremendous union struggle, proving in action that size is not the basic criterion of a revolutionary party's worth.

Events were showing that the Trotskyists possessed the really fundamental revolutionary attributes: program, strategy, tactics, and the fighting capacity to lead workers in battle against the capitalist class. It was the relationship of these considerations to the national party-building activity of the Communist

League that Jim had been quick to see. At the same time his presence in Minneapolis proved helpful to the Teamster comrades in the negotiations for a settlement of the strike.

To give a clear picture of the negotiations it is necessary to backtrack a bit. On the eve of the strike, Local 574 withdrew the closed-shop demand around which the bosses had built up their antiunion propaganda. Instead, the local asked for simple recognition of its legal right to represent the union membership in collective bargaining, a right that was purportedly guaranteed under Section 7(a) of the NRA. The Regional Labor Board had no alternative but to endorse the legitimacy of this modest demand for union recognition. Caught by surprise, the bosses avoided any discussion of the subject, simply ignoring the Labor Board while they tried to figure out a new propaganda line. As a result, the central issue in the strike became clear to the whole city. Everyone could see that the union was merely demanding its legal rights, at the same time being reasonable and flexible about the form of recognition, and that the bosses refused to recognize the the union in any way whatever. Thus the shift in union tactics had outflanked the Citizens Alliance strategists on the propaganda front and added new dimensions to mass support of the strike.

After the walkout began, Governor Olson stepped in as a mediator. Spurning his efforts to get them to meet with the union, the bosses refused to make any concessions whatsoever, and told the governor that it was his duty to use the militia to help them resume their trucking operations. On the union's side it was, of course, logical to cooperate with Olson in his mediation efforts. However, a complication arose due to the differences within the Local 574 leadership. Cliff Hall and executive-board members influenced by him, along with the general run of AFL officials, were inclined to give the governor a free hand in any negotiations. This danger was only partially offset by the presence of Miles Dunne and Bill Brown on Local 574's negotiating committee.

A way had to be found to demonstrate to Olson himself that no shenanigans could be put over on the union membership. An opportunity came on Saturday, May 19, when our pickets were assaulted by the cops at Bearman Fruit. At the time Olson had a negotiation session going at the Athletic Club in which he was shuttling back and forth between the union and employer committees.

Local 574 addressed a message to the governor which read: "At a mass meeting held at 10 o'clock this morning at Strike Headquarters, our members instructed us to make the following ultimatum: A special survey was made by members of the Strike Committee of the situation on the market. After we have been informed that the cops were brutally breaking the heads of our workers with the use of clubs, blackjacks, and lead pipes. We have twelve men seriously and maybe fatally injured in the hospital. We are protesting this violence and unless the Governor instructs the Heads of the Police Department to call the cops off our necks, we will refuse to go on with this conference. Failing to enforce this, Mr. Governor, we will throw our entire force with instructions into the battle and will refuse to arbitrate or negotiate until there is a decisive conclusion in the situation. We will throw out a general call for every worker in Minneapolis and vicinity to assist us in protecting our rights and lives. Pending your action and reply, our delegates to this conference are hereby withdrawn."

If the message had grammatical flaws, it should be kept in mind that it was written hastily under conditions of great tension. Certainly there was no weakness or ambiguity about the contents. As soon as the message had been approved by the membership, a couple of the union's special cruising squads were assigned to deliver it to the governor personally at the Athletic Club and to bring the union negotiators back to strike headquarters. Both assignments were carried out promptly and firmly. The governor had gotten his warning, as had his cronies within the AFL officialdom, and the experience had a salutary effect on Local 574's negotiating committee. In addition, it was a useful way to help the workers understand they couldn't rely upon Olson as mediator.

On Tuesday, May 22, shortly after the truce was declared, the Labor Board came forward with a proposal to settle the strike. Olson called a conference that evening at the Nicollet Hotel to get negotiations started on the basis of the Labor Board proposal. A large force of cruising picket squads escorted the union committee to the hotel. When they got there they found the place swarming with police and another ultimatum was sent inside to the governor: "We refuse to meet with you or discuss any settlement unless you take the cops off our neck." The union's action prevented the springing of a trap prepared by the Citizens Alliance, as we learned later when news leaked out that the cops had warrants for the ar-

rest of the Local 574 negotiators. Olson arranged for the police to be withdrawn; negotiations got under way in indirect
form, the union and employer committees being in separate
rooms, with the governor acting as a go-between.

Three days of hard bargaining followed. In the end the
bosses agreed to recognize the union in the indirect form of
a Labor Board consent order, which upon the union's acceptance was signed by 166 employers in the general trucking industry. After trying unsuccessfully to exclude pickets
convicted of alleged "crimes" during the walkout, the bosses
agreed unconditionally to the reinstatement of all strikers to
their regular jobs. They promised not to discriminate against
workers because of their union membership, and agreed to deal
with representatives of Local 574 on specific matters concerning its individual members. A seniority system was established
to prevent the bosses from weeding out union members. In
general, the form of recognition was sufficiently firm to give
the union a solid basis from which to move forward in a fight
to win steady improvements in wages and conditions.

At one point the negotiations almost foundered on the question of the scope of union recognition. The bosses said flatly
that inside workers would not be included, and thereupon
the union negotiators walked out of the conference, returning
to the strike headquarters. Soon the governor's chauffeur arrived at the headquarters, saying that Olson wanted them
to return to the conference in his limousine to consider a new
proposal on the question. The new formulation extended union
recognition to drivers, helpers, and "such other persons as
are ordinarily engaged in trucking operations."

The key term in this formulation was "operations" related
to trucking, since such operations reached inside the establishments employing drivers and helpers. Because job classifications within these establishments varied considerably according to the type of business, there was a certain advantage
in having a somewhat abstract definition of the scope of union
representation. In every case where such categories of employees were organized, the union could automatically claim its
right to represent them. That was why Local 574 used the
blanket term "inside workers." Substitution of an alternate formulation made no big difference, provided the recognition
clause was understood to include all members of the union.
Olson assured the union negotiators that it did, intimating
that he was merely trying to give the employers a face-saving

formula. On the basis of the governor's guarantee, the union accepted the formulation.

Prior to the strike, the employers generally had raised the truck drivers' pay to fifty cents an hour and comparable increases had been given to other key workers. Their aim was to defuse the organizing campaign and head off a walkout, but the scheme backfired. A clause was included in the agreement that these already significant pay increases must be continued for at least one year. Provision was also made for post-strike negotiation or arbitration of further wage adjustments. A seven-member arbitration board was established, consisting of two Local 574 and two employer representatives, one labor and one employer member of the Regional Labor Board, and the six to name a seventh "neutral" person. It was agreed that hours of labor would remain for the time being as then set by the NRA codes.

On Friday evening, May 25, the proposed settlement was submitted to the union membership with a recommendation from the leadership that it be accepted. Unlike the snake-oil seller's pitch with which the AFL officials had presented the coal settlement the previous February, this proposal was frankly described as a compromise with the bosses. What it did and did not accomplish with respect to the original union demands was forthrightly and fully discussed at the May 25 meeting. Recognizing that they had won a limited victory, primarily in the foundation laid by gaining union recognition, the strikers voted to accept the settlement. On the following morning all went back to work, except the cab drivers.

The main taxi employer, the Yellow Cab Company, was acting independently of the trucking bosses. After the trucking settlement, Yellow Cab began serious negotiations with the union and on June 4 a one-year agreement was signed. Important wage gains were registered and the workers were on the way to establishing union control on the job. Soon the union embraced other taxi workers besides drivers, including starters, telephone operators, garage floor men, baggage drivers, and helpers. Independent taxi drivers obtained a similar agreement. After the settlement a meeting of all the city's taxi drivers voted almost unanimously to stay in Local 574. This action had the effect of liquidating the tiny union of independent taxi owners and their relief drivers which had previously existed. Once again, Tobin's organizational norms were being reversed.

As the victorious workers returned to their jobs, the Communist Party, which had played no part in the struggle, attacked the strike settlement as a "Trotskyite sellout" to the Citizens Alliance. The Stalinists were then on an ultraleft binge. This was a switch from their pre-1928 line of conciliating reformist union bureaucrats and collaborating with capitalist politicians, a course to which they were to return in 1935. Stalinist tactics in 1934 stemmed from their so-called third-period line which had been promulgated at the Sixth Congress of the Communist International in 1928. It was based on predictions that economic crises in the capitalist countries would cause revolutionary situations to spring up virtually overnight. With that expectation the Stalinists charted a sectarian course to give the masses "revolutionary" leadership. As openers they set out to split the labor movement internationally and reorganize it under Communist Party control.

In this country the Communist Party cadres were directed to split the AFL on an utterly artificial basis, sucking whatever workers they could into their adventurous course. Their aim was to build a "red" federation of labor, which ironically enough, they called the Trade Union Unity League. In practice the "red" unions remained paper organizations with few members other than the Stalinists themselves and their direct followers. These "revolutionary" setups were unable even to win recognition from an employer, to say nothing of leading a struggle for power. As a consequence of this ultraleftism and the adventurism attending it, the CP cadres were isolated from the living class struggle. In Minneapolis they had no influence whatever in Local 574. They were left with no alternative but to seek a way to muscle in on the union action from the outside, using mimeographed propaganda material for the purpose.

At the May 15 meeting where Local 574 voted to go on strike the Stalinists appeared with leaflets denouncing Carl Skoglund and the Dunne brothers as "traitors" and "agents of the bosses." During the walkout they demanded, as a price for their support to the union, that agents of their paper organizations be included on the strike committee. When the demand was rejected, they put out more leaflets denouncing the union leadership as "undemocratic." The strikers were so angered by the attack that they would have assaulted the CP distributors if the union leaders had not intervened to prevent it. Bill Brown, who was adept at coining a pithy phrase, said, "The Communist Party has discredited the mimeograph machine."

After the strike was over, Earl Browder, who was then general secretary of the CP, came to Minneapolis and made a public attack on the settlement. The main hatchet job, however, was assigned to William F. Dunne, an older brother of Ray, Miles, and Grant. In the 1928 split, Bill Dunne, who had previously belonged to the Cannon group within the Communist Party, elected to stay with the Stalinists. Now the CP hacks were demanding that he prove his loyalty to them by undertaking the dirty job of attacking his brothers in Local 574. He accepted the assignment. Writing in the CP paper, the *Daily Worker,* Bill Dunne asserted, "The exposure and defeat of Olson should have been the central political objective of the Minneapolis struggle." He attacked the union leadership for making a compromise settlement with the bosses instead of holding out for a "sweeping victory." A general strike should have been proclaimed, he insisted, "over the heads of the AFL officials." On these grounds he charged that the strike had been "defeated" and "betrayed."

Answering the attack in the columns of *The Militant,* Jim Cannon pointed out that, unlike the muddleheaded Stalinists, the workers correctly understood the "central objective" to be recognition of the union. Consequently, an attempt to call a general strike for the "exposure and defeat of Olson" would also have been "over the heads" of the workers. The facts were that the workers had seen the government in operation and they had learned some practical lessons. As in the coal strike, they found the police lined up solidly on the side of the bosses. Olson's mobilization of the militia had been understood as a threat against the strike—a realization that would prove helpful to the union later on. The real central objective of the strike was explained by Jim Cannon in *The Militant* of June 16, 1934.

"It is self-understood that the struggle for economic demands is indissolubly joined with the fight for a union," he wrote, "*but the union is the instrument of the fight* and the guardian of the economic concessions. Every worker who joins the union understands this instinctively. The worker wants an improvement in his conditions, but he wants also security in his job while fighting for these improvements. That is what the formula 'recognition of the union' means concretely. . . . Every strike settlement is a compromise in the sense that it leaves the bosses

in control of industry and free to exploit the workers. The
best settlement only limits and checks this exploitation to a
certain extent. Realistic leaders do not expect justice from the
capitalists, they only strive to extract as much as possible
for the union in the given situation and strengthen their forces
for another fight."

Concerning the provision for arbitration of wage rates, he
added: "This is a serious concession which the union officials
felt it necessary to make under the circumstances in order to
secure the recognition of the union and consolidate it in the
next period. . . . An adverse ruling of the board of arbitration would undoubtedly galvanize the union membership for
action again. The board will meet under the direct impression of the 10-day strike and with the consciousness that the
union is strong and militant. That, in our opinion, is the fundamentally decisive feature of the results of the Minneapolis
strike—the indubitable establishment of a new union where
none existed before. All the plans of the leaders and organizers
were directed to this end as the first objective in a long campaign. The struggle was centered around the issue and was
crowned with success. On that basis further steps forward can
be made. To speak of such an outcome as a 'defeat' is simply
absurd."

Jim Cannon's appraisal of the outcome of the strike was
shared generally by the workers involved. As they returned
to their jobs Local 574 buttons were proudly displayed
throughout the trucking industry. Filling-station attendants,
with whom there had been considerable trouble during the
strike, began to join the union. There was also a steady influx
of package-delivery drivers, some of whom had tried to scab
early in the walkout.

Before long Local 574 had over 7,000 members, and it
continued to gain new recruits daily. Job committees were
set up to handle grievances and collect union dues. Besides
this, the size of the union and the scope of its activities now
required a staff of full-time organizers. On June 1, the executive board adopted a motion by Moe Hork to assign this
function to Ray, Miles, and Grant Dunne, Carl Skoglund, and
myself at salaries of twenty-five dollars a week, the average
wage of truck drivers. The action was another step toward
according official status to what had become the real leadership of the union.

Our first task as organizers was to deal with poststrike griev-

ances which could not be settled by the union committees on
the job. These included surprisingly few refusals to put strikers
back to work. In most cases the individual bosses showed
a readiness to meet with union representatives and settle the
dispute.

In one case Ray Dunne and I, who were working together
on the union staff, had a bizarre experience. A market firm
had made a deal with a competitor to split a carload of
oranges that was to be unloaded at the regular starting time
of a certain work day. Then the boss ordered one of his drivers
to get there early and haul away something more than his
half of the carload. The driver refused, saying that he now
belonged to a union and he didn't have to do things like that
anymore. He was fired for "insubordination." We gave the
boss the alternative of putting the man back or facing a strike.
He just sat back and looked at us for a few moments and
you could see in his eyes that he was reviewing the scene of
the fighting in the market. Then he decided to return the driver
to his job.

About mid-June the grievance situation suddenly changed.
It resulted from Citizens Alliance pressure on the bosses to
discriminate against union members by chiseling on wage
rates and firing them in violation of their seniority. Within
a short time over 700 cases of such discrimination piled up;
the union met stubborn refusals in most instances to make
any redress of the workers' grievances. Clearly the Citizens
Alliance was looking for a new opening to challenge the union.

This intention was made doubly plain by the attitude of
the employer committee when the union sought through the
Labor Board to negotiate or arbitrate further wage increases
in accord with the provisions of the strike settlement. The employer representatives hemmed and hawed, saying neither yes
nor no, and nothing happened. With the Labor Board failing to enforce the terms of settlement, the union tried to deal
directly with the bosses as individuals. They referred us to
their committee, saying they couldn't act on their own. Meantime they were handing out a few piecemeal wage increases
with the aim of creating dissension in the union ranks.

Only one thing was plainly stated by the employer representatives. They refused to deal with the union concerning
inside workers, saying that they were empowered to bargain
with Local 574 simply on matters relating to truck drivers
and helpers. Their intent was to split the union membership

by inducing the drivers and helpers to turn their backs on the inside workers. Such an outcome would minimize the actual gain in union power and limit the scope of any concessions they might have to make to their employees. Having done their homework well, the bosses were fully aware of Tobin's organizational concepts and knew that he would be sympathetic with their stand in limiting the scope of union recognition. Local 574's industrial-union course would be reversed and the union restricted to a narrow craft structure. This would facilitate cleaning out the radical leadership in order to put the local under the control of "labor statesmen."

Such a reversal of the union's course would also have been congenial to Governor Olson's needs, since Local 574's militant struggle had put him on the political hot seat. Being a slick maneuverer, Olson may well have anticipated that a dispute over the scope of representation would follow when he assured the union negotiators that the strike settlement gave full union recognition, including inside workers. Such a probability flows from the obvious fact that his main aim at the time was to get the strikers back to work at all hazards. In any case, he now tried to straddle the issue when the Labor Board asked for his interpretation of the union-representation clause in the settlement. In a letter of June 21, 1934, he suggested that the clause should be construed to include such categories as shipping and receiving clerks, stevedores, and freight-elevator operators. Then he negated even this limited concession to the union by advocating that the final determination be left to arbitration.

Olson's letter brought a harsh response from the bosses, who bought a big newspaper ad in which they claimed that the union had a right to deal for only truck drivers and helpers. Emulating the bosses in brushing aside the governor's statement, the Labor Board handed down an interpretation of the union-recognition clause in the strike settlement. It ruled that the union had the right to represent only drivers, helpers, and platform workers "directly engaged in loading and unloading trucks." The bosses quickly accepted this antilabor decision which denied the union its legal right to represent members employed as inside workers. In a statement rejecting the ruling for the swindle it was, the union added with a touch of irony: "The Labor Board has 'generously' ruled that Local 574 shall have the right to represent almost half of its membership."

Meantime, on the day the governor's letter had been released to the press, Local 574 held a membership meeting to take stock of the deteriorating situation. The meeting voted to press demands for recognition of the union's right to represent all its members and for immediate wage increases. To back up the demands it was decided to begin preparations for another tie-up. At the same time a letter reporting the situation was sent by Cliff Hall to Thomas L. Hughes, general secretary-treasurer of the IBT, written on this occasion in consultation with the rest of the union leadership. As a diplomatic gesture, it was explained that the international executive board had not been asked to sanction the May strike because most of the local's members were new and were not entitled to strike benefits under the IBT bylaws. No mention was made of the new dispute over union representation for inside workers, since both Tobin and Hughes would be cold on that subject. Instead the letter stressed the employers' refusal to arbitrate the wage question as provided in the strike settlement.

Because of the heavy expenses incurred in the strike, a request was made of Hughes that the local be exempted from the initiation-fee tax for the 3,000 new members taken in during May. This was a reasonable request, Hall wrote, "as we feel that we did not derive any benefits from the International during the eleven-day strike." Assurance was given in return that the per capita tax of thirty cents on the monthly membership dues would be paid regularly to the International Union.

In his reply Hughes stated: "The laws of the organization are very plain on this matter and we must receive $1.00 for each man who paid his initiation fee into your local." He said nothing at all about the difficulties the local was having with the employers. As later events will show, when a statement was made on the subject, it came from Tobin himself and took the form of a blow against Local 574.

Turning to a quarter from which help could be counted on in a new battle with the bosses, the union set out to consolidate the women's auxiliary. Since the end of the May strike the auxiliary had been aiding families of pickets who had been injured in the fighting or were still serving terms in the work-house. Now there was an even bigger job of securing economic assistance for the many workers victimized in the new Citizens Alliance offensive against the union. Besides fighting to get them on public relief, the women organized a tag day to secure public donations on behalf of the class-war victims. They also went before other unions seeking contributions. With the threat of another strike looming, there would soon be much more to do and more hands would be needed, so the auxiliary launched a recruiting drive. The response was good, applications for membership even coming from outside Local 574 circles. Once again a key detachment of fighting women was being mobilized for the pending battle, built around the experienced veterans of the May struggle.

Parallel to the union preparations for renewed conflict, the Communist League began to gear itself as a national organization to give all possible support to the Minneapolis Teamsters. To finance the effort a party-wide fund drive was launched. A campaign was also conducted to expand the circulation of *The Militant,* especially by reaching out for subscribers among workers nationally who had been inspired by the May strike.

Once again Jim Cannon came to Minneapolis and in consultation with the local comrades it was decided to bring in some additional party members who were especially qualified to play key assisting roles. These included two top-notch journalists: Max Shachtman and Herbert Solow, who later became an editor of *Fortune.* Albert Goldman, a prominent Chicago labor attorney, came to serve as general counsel for the union. Hugo Oehler, a talented leader of mass actions, soon arrived to help mobilize support for Local 574 among the unemployed.

Several factors served to promote good working relations between these comrades sent to Minneapolis by the national organization and the local party members who were leading the union struggle. As a consequence of Jim's visit in May, the national party leadership could not act with a much surer grasp of the local situation than had previously been the case. At the same time the party fraction in the union was fully aware that valuable help could be received from the comrades who had come to offer special assistance. We were involved in a highly complex struggle, fraught with many hazards of a political nature. As in the case of all modern strikes, we could profit from competent political consultation and the help of journalists who were politically class conscious. It was also invaluable to have the services of an experienced organizer of unemployed workers and an able lawyer who was a revolutionary. These were precisely the main forms of aid received from the comrades the party sent to help us. A new dimension was thereby added to the union's general staff, an accomplishment that was bound to yield important dividends.

As had been the case since action began in the coal industry, members of the local Communist League branch played an important assisting role. Their efforts centered around work in other unions than Local 574, among the unemployed, and in the women's auxiliary. They also strove to build up *The Militant's* readership, thereby serving to promote class consciousness among the workers by means of the paper's political analysis of the union struggle. Those playing outstanding roles in these activities included Fannie Barach, Si Barach, Goldie Cooper, Oscar Coover, Sr., William Curran, C. R. and P. G. Hedlund, Chester Johnson, Louis Roseland, and Joe Ross. Taken as a whole, the local party branch had been gradually increasing in size since the beginning of the organizing drive in coal. A consequent rise of its effectiveness in the labor movement was shown by the fact that most of the new members had been recruited within Local 574, and there was now a substantial party fraction in that union.

An extraordinary effort was made to strengthen Local 574 in the vital sphere of publicity and propaganda. On June 25 the local launched its own newspaper, *The Organizer*. Through this medium the union could refute the lies of the boss press, give the true facts about its own aims and policies, and expose the antilabor schemes of the bosses and the government. The paper was enthusiastically received by the workers, who read it carefully and helped to distribute it widely. At the outset *The Organizer* appeared as a modest semitabloid of four pages with a press run of 5,000. It came out weekly, but plans were made to begin daily publication if the union, as anticipated, was again forced on strike.

I was listed as the editor, even though I was too busy at other tasks to get out a paper and besides I didn't know how to do so at the time. This was done because it was useful to formally name a union leader for the post. The actual editors were Max Shachtman and Herbert Solow, assisted by Carlos Hudson, a local comrade with journalistic ability. Jim Cannon also pitched in on the editorial writing. Editorial policy was decided through joint consultations between the union leaders and the party journalists. With the kind of teamwork that we were able to establish, the union had a powerful new weapon in its arsenal.

THE ORGANIZER

Bulletin of the Strike Committee of 100 and official organ of General Drivers, Helpers, Petroleum and Inside Workers Union, Local 574, affiliated with the American Federation of Labor.

STAFF

Farrell Dobbs .... Fall Guy
Jim McGee .... Office Boy
Carlos ("head ¼ s") Hudson .... End Man
Jerry Hudson .... Artiste
Max Marsh .... St. Paul Correspondent
Albert Goldman .... Mouthpiece
Marvel Dobbs .... Military Reporter
William S. Brown, the Three Dunne Sisters and Carl Skoglund .... Stooges
Herbert Solow .... Guest Conductor

"The first strike daily in American history" — tribute from The Organizer.

FORTY-ONE ISSUES THAT KNOCKED THEM FOR A LOOP!

Published every day but Sunday at 225 South Third St., Minneapolis, Minnesota

SATURDAY, AUGUST 25, 1934

Volume 1, Number 40

The Organizer was the first strike daily ever published by a union in the United States. This joke masthead appeared in the August 25, 1934, issue. James P. Cannon is listed as Jim McGee and Max Shachtman as Max Marsh (a St. Paul correspondent because he and Cannon were driven out of Minneapolis by the National Guard and forced to live in the neighboring city, St. Paul, for a short period of time).

"The Daring Old Gent On the Flying Trapeze"

Minneapolis Communism—42½ Cents an Hour

The Organizer **takes on Citizens Alliance red-baiting.**

The Strike Resumes

With another strike looming as a certainty, attention was turned to shoring up Local 574's alliances. An agreement was reached with three farm organizations: The Farmers' Holiday Association, the National Farm Bureau, and the Market Gardeners Association. It provided that the union pickets would not interfere with farm trucks during the strike if they carried permits from Local 574 and the farm organization to which each operator belonged. To prevent chiseling on this arrangement farmers' committees undertook to picket roads leading into Minneapolis. When put into practice later on, the procedure worked well. Difficulties experienced during the May action were largely avoided, and the union enjoyed general sympathy among the farmers. Sentiment favorable to the union was further enhanced by the fact that the dual character of the permit system enabled the farm organizations to conduct effective recruitment drives of their own.

Since the commission row in the city market would again be closed in the upcoming walkout, it was necessary to keep the market gardeners clear of this potential battle area. Toward that end the union leased a big parking lot a few blocks away from the regular market district. Market gardeners were allowed to use it rent free for their commerce with small grocers, thus giving the gardeners an added incentive to cooperate with us in view of the rents gouged from them on commission row. Small grocers were permitted to pick up produce at the new market in passenger cars, but they were not allowed to use trucks. This presented no problem for them since their purchases were not very bulky. The system proved to be so successful that it was continued even after the next strike was over, and appreciation was shown to the union by donations to its commissary.

Steps were also taken to give further assurance to the unemployed that their alliance with the union would not be a one-sided affair. Local 574 joined in signing a call for a united labor conference on unemployed problems. This action by what had become the city's most respected union helped to emphasize strongly the duty of employed workers to back the demands of the unemployed. It gave fresh impetus to a growing trend toward practical union cooperation with the unemployed in fighting to improve the public relief system.

At the same time Local 574 moved to establish closer organizational coordination with the unemployed in the next strike through the medium of the Minneapolis Central Council of Workers. The MCCW was a delegated body of representatives from various workers' organizations such as unemployed formations, trade unions, labor political groups, workers' fraternal associations, cooperative movements, youth, and women's organizations of a working-class nature. It had been created for the express purpose of fighting in behalf of jobless workers. Arrangements were made for this organization to register volunteers among the unemployed who wanted to support Local 574 in the pending battle with the trucking bosses. They were issued MCCW buttons, which it was understood would give them official picket status under the direction of the union's strike committee.

As in May, special measures were again needed to line up the city's trade-union movement in support of our struggle. A campaign was launched to get public backing from unions in all the various trades. Virtually every member of Local 574 participated in the effort, pressing our case among other rank-and-file unionists and thereby helping to bring pressure on the AFL officialdom. Local 574's leadership was thus enabled to push through an official AFL call for a joint conference of all unions in town. This conference scheduled a united labor march and protest rally against the union-busting tactics of the trucking bosses, to be held on July 6, 1934.

By 6:00 P. M. on the evening of the demonstration, working people gathering for the parade filled the marshaling area in the Bridge Square district. For over an hour steady streams of men and women continued to pour in, forming columns that extended along adjacent streets. At 7:30 the head of the parade swung up Nicollet Avenue, a principal thoroughfare in the heart of the city, on the eighteen-block march to the Municipal Auditorium where the protest rally was held. A squadron of motorcycle couriers from the May strike made sure that the way ahead was cleared for the marchers, who

were led by Grand Marshal Ed Hudson, a Farmer-Labor
Party alderman. The union had obtained a fine horse for
Hudson to ride. This seemed to please him greatly and we,
too, were happy about it because such a prominent display
of support would make it harder for him to chicken out on
us when the going got rough. He was followed by a band
from the musicians' union.

Then came Local 574, the ranks of its long column striding
proudly under the union's banner. Behind us marched the
women's auxiliary, other Teamster locals, the building trades,
streetcar workers, printers, brewers, railroad workers, machin-
ists, unemployed organizations, laundry workers, upholsterers,
city and county employees, garment workers, and other labor
contingents, including a detachment of trade unionists from
St. Paul, an adjacent city. Members of the Farmers' Holiday
Association also marched with us, as did a number of students
from the University of Minneasota. Banners carried in the
parade proclaimed: "We support 574"; "Down With The Citizens Alliance"; and "Down With the Red Baiters." Two small
planes bearing Local 574's insignia circled overhead. They
belonged to sympathizers who volunteered them for the union's
use in sending representatives about the state to appeal for aid.
Over 6,000 onlookers, mostly sympathetic, flanked the line
of march and the rolling advance of especially loud cheers
from them marked the progress of Local 574's passage up the
avenue.

Picket captains from the May strike monitored the parade,
and they firmly enforced the union ruling that those who
marched would be the first to enter the auditorium for the
protest rally. By the time the rally began, over 12,000 were
packed into the auditorium, and thousands more stood outside listening to the loudspeakers. A. H. Urtabees, president
of the Building Trades Council, presided over the meeting.
Roy Wier spoke for the Central Labor Union, Emery Nelson
for the Teamsters Joint Council, and Robert Fleming for the
St. Paul Teamsters Unions. John Bosch of the Farmers' Holiday Association pledged support to Local 574 on behalf of
the farmers. The union speakers stressed that the trucking
bosses had broken the May agreement with Local 574, calling
this a challenge on the part of the Citizens Alliance that had
to be met by the entire labor movement. Bill Brown and Miles
Dunne spoke for Local 574.

As recorded in a stenographer's transcript of the meeting,

Miles Dunne answered a smear attack on the union leadership which had been launched by the bosses, saying: "They have now raised the red issue and accused us of being reds and radicals . . . of wanting to substitute a new form of government and I say to you here frankly . . . when a system of society exists that allows employers in Minneapolis to wax fat on the misery and starvation and degradation of the many, it is time that system is changed, it is high time that the workers take this from their hands and take for themselves at least a fair share of all the wealth they produce."

Bill Brown declared: "I say tonight, and say we should go on record, that either this union movement is going to move out or else the Citizens Alliance, and we like this place [Very heavy applause.]. . . . I want to say there is not a fair employer unless we are burying them [Laughter from the crowd.]. . . . I contend this, that the working class, they are the taxpayers. We don't want to have our agency, the Police Department, used against us. If they do, if they do, God damn it, we have enough people to remove the Police Department."

Without a dissenting voice the rally adopted a resolution containing four main points: that Local 574 had the right to represent all its members; that all the local's members should get a wage increase retroactive to May 26; that the bosses must sign a written agreement with the union; and that a deadline for compliance with these demands be set for Wednesday, July 11. Thus spoke the massive single-issue coalition, united around the slogan, "Make Minneapolis a Union Town."

At precisely this high point in the labor mobilization for struggle against the Citizens Alliance, Tobin hurled a poisoned dart at Local 574. It struck in the form of editorials in the July 1934 issue of the official IBT magazine. In one editorial, written primarily to take a crack at Congressman Shoemaker because of the telegram he had authored during the May strike, Tobin declared the May walkout to be "in violation of all our laws." In another item he asserted: "No matter how much a few radicals in our union may rave about the laws of the International, let it be distinctly understood now, until our laws are changed, this International Union will not sanction a sympathetic strike, nor will it in any way, shape or manner, approve the violation of a signed contract. As I have repeatedly stated . . . unless we keep our contracts and protect ourselves, we would be continuously in trouble on account of the inside workers, or others, going out on strike."

Really venting his spleen, Tobin wrote in the lead editorial: "We see from the newspapers that the infamous Dunn[e] Brothers . . . were very prominent in the strike of Local No. 574 of Minneapolis. . . . All we can say to our people is to beware of these wolves in sheep clothing. . . . Never was there freedom in any country for the workers equal to that enjoyed by the workers of this country. That freedom is liable to be endangered by those semi-monsters who are creeping into our midst and getting into some of our newly organized local unions, creating distrust, discontent, bloodshed and rebellion. The officers of local unions who do not guard themselves and their unions against a human monster of this kind are making a mistake. If you love the union which you have worked to build up, get busy and stifle such radicals, because they do not belong in the union. . . . This International Union cannot watch them, but you men, who are closely in touch with your membership, should be on the watch for them and, believe me, when we find out that you are after one of the mob of hounds described above, the International Union will help you in every way it can . . . to protect our people from these serpents in human form."

What a propaganda package Tobin had handed to the bosses! Inside workers made "trouble" for truck drivers. Local 574's impending walkout, like the May strike, would obviously be deemed "in violation of all our laws." Other Teamster locals were warned against taking sympathetic action in support of the walkout. Radical "monsters" were blamed for the bloodshed in May, a truly monstrous statement that indicted the union in advance for whatever violence the bosses chose next to use against it. A purge of the Local 574 leadership was urged, and Tobin promised to help do the dirty job.

Eagerly grabbing this apostate's gift from the head of the IBT, the bosses republished Tobin's editorials as a paid ad in the *Minneapolis Daily Star* of July 7, 1934. Some of the more scurrilous terms used by Tobin were coyly left out, with an explanatory note that "Words omitted are not acceptable for newspaper use." The ad appeared the day after the huge labor demonstration in support of Local 574. It was then reproduced in leaflet form by the bosses for mass distribution among the workers. Ad and leaflet alike were headlined: "Communists and radicals in local unions, says President Tobin." Aided by this windfall from Tobin, the Citizens Alliance now went all out in its smear attack on the union. Taking a tip from Stalinist red-baiting of Local 574 leadership, the bosses' attack centered on "Trotsky Communists." It was charged that the Trotskyists were out to make a revolution in Minneapolis, not to build a union. Unctuously deploring harm done to "legitimate unions," the Citizens Alliance called for support against "Communist-led" Local 574.

At this juncture, E. H. Dunnigan, a "Commissioner of Conciliation" from the U. S. Department of Labor, stepped into the picture. Probably at Olson's suggestion, he soon appeared at Local 574's headquarters which had been moved after the May strike to 225 South Third Street. His visit was described by Marvel Scholl in a diary she kept at the time: "Today the federal mediator — I am almost tempted to say meditator, as Harry DeBoer calls them — arrived in town. Mr. Dunnigan. I don't believe he had any idea of the situation here when he came to town. Pompously he came to headquarters — and deflated he left! And Mac [Mrs. McCormack] and I had our share in the deflation. It was early in the afternoon while we were working on the order for our hospital at the new strike headquarters that a short, fat, elegantly dressed creature, replete with four fat cigars in his coat pocket, pince-nez glasses with a wide black ribbon dangling to his lapel and a huge umbrella, suddenly thrust himself upon us. 'I'm Dunnigan, federal mediator. I wish to see the organizing committee,' he announced, leaning on the umbrella. 'They are busy right now,' he was told. 'Do you care to wait?'

"Impatiently he seated himself. 'Will you announce me?' he demanded. 'Oh yes,' we told him. And we announced him. Returning with instructions that the committee would be able to see Mr. Dunnigan in fifteen minutes, Mac eased herself back into her chair and, with a twinkle in her eyes which presaged fun, proceded to dictate a list of supplies for the hospital which would have sufficed for a six month civil war. Mr. Dunnigan's eyes began to pop. He sweated, he squirmed, but we went right ahead. Mac made comments as she enlarged the order, specifying instances where we might need the item mentioned. And Mr. Dunnigan continued to sweat, squirm and tap his umbrella on the floor. At last someone came out to usher him into the meeting. Mac and I laughed until our sides ached, and then went back to our real work."

In the session with the union leadership Dunnigan tried to create the impression that he was secretly on our side. On that basis he asked us to authorize him to make "minor" concessions

to the bosses concerning the union demands, stressing that he
needed such leeway for "bargaining purposes." We flatly rejected the request, pegging it for what it was, a con game calculated to make suckers of the workers. After informing him
of what the workers wanted from the employers, we suggested
that he go see what he could do about getting some action from
them. It was also pointed out that a July 11 deadline had been
set, at which time the union intended to go on strike if the bosses persisted in the attitude they had taken. Dunnigan pleaded
for a five-day extension of the deadline, and that much alone
was granted to him.

As had been previously scheduled, Local 574 held a membership meeting on July 11. Although nothing had come of
Dunnigan's talks with the employers since our session with him,
we kept our promise to extend the deadline for five days. The
meeting decided, by a standing vote, to go on strike for en-
forcement of the union demands on Monday, July 16, at twelve
midnight.

The strike call, which was unanimously adopted, summed up
the general situation: All efforts to establish living wages and
improve working conditions had been frustrated by the arrogant
attitude of the employers. By its failure to act, the Labor Board
had upheld the hand of these employers. The right of the union
to represent all its members had been denied. Personal attacks
were made on the union leaders in an effort by the bosses to
dictate who should speak for the workers. Red-baiting had
been dragged in as a fraudulent maneuver to divert attention
from the real issues in the dispute.

Angry words were also directed at the general president of
the IBT in the strike call: "We say plainly to D. J. Tobin: If
you can't act like a Union man, and help us, instead of helping the bosses, then at least have the decency to stand aside
and let us fight our battle alone. We did it in the organization
campaign and in the previous strike and we can do it again.
We received absolutely no help of any kind from you. Our
leadership and guidance has come from our local leaders,
and them alone. We put our confidence in them and will not
support any attack on them under any circumstances."

The Citizens Alliance quickly reacted to the strike call, again
using Tobin's editorials as ammunition for a stepped-up smear
campaign against Local 574. His disapproval of the May
walkout was emphasized. Then this boss outfit impudently
attacked the local for making the July 11 strike decision by

standing vote, instead of taking a secret ballot as "provided for in the [union] by-laws." These sharpies tried to make it appear scandalous that women were at the union meeting, hoping people would not realize that they were members of the auxiliary. Local 574 officials were castigated for attacking Tobin at the meeting, "because he fearlessly exposed the Communist leadership" of the union.

To help "Fearless Dan" in this exposure, a Citizens Alliance bulletin came up with some choice tidbits: "It has already been pointed out that five of the paid organizers of General Drivers' Union, Local #574, are reliably reported to be the moving spirits in the Minneapolis branch of the Communist League of America, which is sponsoring the program of the Fourth Internationale [sic]; viz., a dictatorship of the proletariat. . . . V. R. Dunne and Carl Skoglund, organizers of the union . . . are reported to be on the National Committee of the Communist League of America."

The same bulletin also quoted from Bill Brown's speech in presenting the resolution adopted at the July 6 labor rally at the Municipal Auditorium, the bulletin's editor supplying the underlining of passages in the quotation: "Before I read this resolution— *it is a revolution in fact*— I want to say that we are going to take a rising vote, and I don't want to see one person sitting down. *I would like to turn this assembly loose on the Citizens Alliance in the morning.*"

This propaganda assault was designed to split the labor coalition formed in support of Local 574 and to cause a rupture within the local itself. We undertook prompt measures to ward off these twin dangers. Within Local 574 a joint meeting of the organizing committee and executive board was held to stiffen the spine of the latter body and again put it on record in support of a showdown fight with the bosses. At that session a resolution was adopted to schedule another general membership meeting on Monday evening, July 16, for the following purposes: to reaffirm the strike call adopted on July 11; to take a secret ballot on the strike so that the membership could demonstrate its sentiments finally and conclusively; and to elect a strike committee of 100 to conduct the strike. In addition the executive board unanimously declared full confidence in the organizing committee, called upon its members to remain at their posts, and asked the union membership to confirm this declaration.

A report of these actions was published in *The Organizer,*

along with the full text of Local 574's strike call. This show of solidarity within the embattled local made it possible to get reaffirmations of support, first from the Building Trades Council and then from the Central Labor Union.

Meanwhile the bosses had come up with another diabolical ploy, an attempt to engineer a "split" of inside market workers from Local 574. A handful of men were duped into signing a call for a rump meeting at Wesley Church on Sunday, July 15, to launch a movement for a "noncommunist" union. About 500 attended the rump affair, the overwhelming majority of them being loyal members of Local 574. A Reverend William Brown—not a relative of the union president—tried to open the meeting but he couldn't make himself heard. Grant Dunne mounted the platform, took charge of the proceedings and denounced the preacher and the other stooges of the bosses for their underhanded efforts to split the union. A motion expressing confidence in the union leadership was then adopted, and thus the meeting intended to demoralize the workers turned into a demonstration in support of Local 574.

On the following evening, July 16, the union held its officially scheduled meeting at Eagles Hall. It was a hot night and the hall was packed with sweltering workers who were in a fighting mood. In response to a motion presented by Moe Hork, the membership unanimously voted full confidence in the leaders, proving the boss propaganda about an "anticommunist" revolt within the union to be a fake. Bill Brown, Miles Dunne, and I then spoke, bringing the membership up to date on developments and advocating reaffirmation of the July 11 strike decision. As presiding officer, Brown urged that any present who opposed the walkout take the floor and express their views. No one did so. When the question was put before the body, the workers brushed aside the proposal to take a secret ballot and decided unanimously by standing vote to go on strike forthwith.

After a strike committee of 100 had been elected, the meeting ended with spontaneous singing of the union song, "Solidarity." We then adjourned to the new strike headquarters, a two-story garage building at 215 South Eighth Street, only to find that the Citizens Alliance had induced the landlord to lock us out. As indignant tenants who had paid their rent, the strikers broke into the building and began preparations for Tuesday morning's action. The garage, by the way, was across the street from the Minneapolis Club, a swank setup patronized by the "best families." They were to have some shocking experiences in the weeks ahead.

The strike committee, which served as a broad executive formation during the walkout, was not just a happenstance aggregate of 100. It was composed of militants to whom the membership had accorded leadership recognition because of their roles in the February and May struggles. As a result this democratically elected body was genuinely representative of the union rank and file. Close ties consequently existed between membership and leadership based on mutual understanding, confidence, and trust forged in the heat of battle.

Within the strike committee as a whole a central leadership formation was structured. It took shape around a nucleus consisting of the union's five full-time organizers — Ray, Miles, and Grant Dunne, Carl Skoglund, and myself. As union president, Bill Brown worked closely with us. This guiding formation also contained a strong component of secondary leaders, some of whom had come forward during the May conflict to take their places alongside veterans of the coal strike. As part of the leadership team they proved their worth time and time again at critical junctures. Experience in the class struggle and education gained in the course of battle led a number of them to join the Communist League. LEFT-WING UNION GOVT

In general terms, relations between the strike committee and the union ranks were somewhat akin to the Leninist concept of democratic centralism: democracy in reaching decisions; discipline in carrying them out. Policy decisions and leadership selections were made through full and free discussion at union membership meetings. During actual combat with the bosses, on the other hand, decisions by the leaders were to be carried out without argument. When a given action was over such decisions were, of course subject to review and criticism by the membership. These norms applied not only to relations between the strike committee and the union ranks; they applied also to leadership relations within the broad strike committee itself. All in all, the union's structural and procedural norms served as the warp and woof for an internal unity that made it a formidable fighting machine.

With this new stage of internal union development further steps became possible to minimize the difficulties caused by the incompetence of the official executive board. In effect, the board was temporarily stripped of all authority. This was done by first making all members of the board and the busi-

ness agent, Cliff Hall, a part of the strike committee. Then
the latter body, as recorded in the minutes of its first session,
adopted a motion that read: "Strike committee to be executive
body in the strike, with full power to make any and all decisions." At the same meeting the committee of 100 took steps to
avoid a repetition of previous difficulties with Hall and the
executive board in the matter of negotiations with the bosses.
It passed a motion which decreed: "The contact committee to
meet with the employers shall be small, their only function
to be that of meeting with the employers. All their actions are
subject to ratification of the strike committee." Ray Dunne and
I were elected as a contact committee of two.

Several things about the meaning of this decision are worth
noting. When serving as negotiators, AFL officials usually
took it upon themselves to decide what terms the union would
accept, and then they would shove their decision down the
throats of the membership. To make clear that this wouldn't
be tolerated, the designation "contact committee" was used, instead of employing the term "negotiating committee." In addition the committee was made a small one, formally because
of its restricted function, but also to keep Hall and his kind
off of it. These considerations were not the only reasons for
the decision.

It is a mistake under any circumstances for union negotiators to deal with bosses or government mediators on the
basis that they have authority to make a compromise. Once
a concession has been made under heavy pressure, which
comes especially from the boss-controlled government agents,
the action can be reversed only with the greatest difficulty,
if at all. A virtually irreparable injustice can thereby be done
to the union membership. If a statement is made as to the
minimum the union negotiators will recommend, it also automatically defines the maximum the bosses will offer. Consequently, whenever any question of a compromise arises,
negotiators should always say they will have to take the matter
back to the union for a decision. This procedure is not only
a safeguard against bureaucratic malpractice, it is the best
course for union representatives who want to do the right
thing. For these general reasons it was proper from every
viewpoint to require that all actions by Local 574's negotiators be subject to control by the strike committee of 100.

In several additional respects the union was able to add
improvements in preparing for the strike, profiting from the

May experiences. The commissary was better organized and more efficiently operated, its larder better stocked with foodstuffs donated by farmers and merchants. Advances were registered in setting up the union hospital, again under the supervision of Dr. McCrimmon, and Mrs. McCormack. Arrangements were made for a top-notch legal staff. It consisted of Albert Goldman, Fred Ossanna, a prominent local attorney, and Irving Green, a junior member of Ossanna's legal firm. As in May, nightly meetings were held at the strike headquarters for the workers to hear reports on the day's events, listen to guest speakers, and enjoy some form of entertainment.

At the first strike committee meeting, chaired by Kelly Postal, the question of "picketing equipment" was put on the agenda. For the first time since the truce toward the end of the May strike, the bosses would be trying to operate trucks in defiance of the pickets. The last attempt had been stopped when the strikers won a pitched battle with the cops, fought club against club. At this new juncture many pickets were inclined to start where they left off in May, again arming themselves with clubs. In the changed circumstances, however, this would have been tactically inadvisable. It would have given the cops a pretext for immediate violence against strikers who were trying to peacefully picket; and the union would have lost the tactical advantage of reacting to police violence under defensive slogans.

The decision on this point was recorded in the minutes of a strike committee meeting held at 12:30 A.M. on July 17: "The Chair then brought the question of picket equipment before the meeting. Dobbs then arose and requested that, if there be any violence, let it not be said that 574 started it, and that . . . going out on picket duty armed at this time would only create trouble. It was suggested that all picket equipment be brought to headquarters and kept there. By general agreement this suggestion of Dobbs' was accepted."

Picketing was organized in two shifts of twelve hours, and Kelly Postal, acting in consultation with Ray Dunne, Harry DeBoer, and me, served as chief picket dispatcher. Marvel Scholl recorded impressions of Postal in her diary: "Kelly has peculiar eyes. They are at once, soft and steely. His success as a general in 574's army can be atrributed in part to his ability to judge a man accurately almost at once." She also descirbed the ordinary dispatching routine: "Cars line the driveway. Each returning picket crew drives through the parking lot to the rear of the garage, to take its place in a line which extends through the garage to the front door. Sometimes there is a wait, but most of the time an incoming car reaches the door in a hurry. The picket dispatcher whispers the destination in the driver's ear." The latter practice, which involved the use of a code in dispatching pickets, had been ordered by the strike committee. It was a procedure that had been developed during the May strike to cope with problems created by provocateurs.

Sentiment was expressed in the strike committee to force other Teamster locals immediately on strike in support of Local 574. After some discussion the counsel offered by Carl Skoglund prevailed. By intelligent cooperation with them at the present stage, he argued, the various Teamster crafts could better be induced later, if necessary, to give full and willing support to Local 574. It was decided to exempt ice, milk, bakery, brewery, and city-owned trucks, if operated by union drivers. Taxis were allowed to operate since the union now had a direct contract with the owners. For tactical reasons oil trucks and filling stations were exempted from the strike in view of the fact that the oil companies were negotiating with the union. Beyond that only individual exceptions were made when recommended by the union's complaint committee, chaired by Ray Rainbolt. He was an ideal person for the assignment, capable of fairness toward the deserving, but deaf to the wheedling of petty chiselers.

The general policy followed is reflected in the strike committee minutes of July 19, recording a report by Rainbolt: "Permit to city [requested] for gravel on the asphalt job — he recommended no permit. Permit requested for fish company to move fish to Camp Riley [a military installation] — no permit. Dental Supply Co. request for a motorcycle permit—no permit. New trucks to be used as a display at World's Fair in Chicago — request permitted." These decisions reported by Rainbolt were approved by the strike committee to the accompaniment of sarcastic references to the gall of the city fathers and the army. International Harvester was the firm involved in moving the new trucks to the World's Fair. In return for the permit it agreed that they would be paraded through town with big signs reading, "Moved with Local 574's permission." The company also made a donation to the union's commissary. As usual, Rainbolt had driven a hard bargain.

As in February and May, Local 574 swiftly demonstrated the ability to enforce its rulings. On the first day of the strike—

Tuesday, July 17 — the city's streets were devoid of trucks other than those the union permitted to operate. An attempt was made on the second day to move trucks in the market, but the bosses soon backed off from the effort when they were confronted with a formidable picket concentration. By this time, however, the cops were stepping up their intervention, making the first arrests of pickets for "disorderly conduct." It was the opening gambit of a new flareup of civil strife that was soon to rage with greater violence than had occurred in May.

Governor Olson also intervened earlier than he had in the previous conflict, once again trying at the outset to straddle the issue. At the request of Mayor Bainbridge he mobilized the National Guard for the "preservation of law and order," meanwhile assuring the union that he would not take sides in the strike.

The union paper, *The Organizer,* blasted Olson for his action in its issue of July 18. It pointed out that the troop display could have only one purpose: intimidation and coercion aimed at the union. This move against the strike took place at a time when the only threat to public peace came from the bosses' use of scabs, thugs, and deputized hoodlums. Such action meant the governor was already taking sides against the workers. He was not even being neutral, which in itself would also be a violation of his duty to his labor constituency. Olson was reminded that he owed his high post to support from workers and farmers. They had a right to expect support from him in their struggles, not the threat of military force against them. *The Organizer* demanded immediate withdrawal of the troops, declaring: "No truck is going to be moved! By nobody!"

On Monday, July 16, the day before the strike began, *The Organizer* had been converted to a daily and the paper continued on that basis for the duration of the walkout. *It was the first strike daily ever published by a union in the United States.* A weekly paper would have been utterly inadequate to deal with the fast-moving events. Daily publication, on the other hand, enabled the union to break the capitalist monopoly of the press, thereby cutting through the propaganda screen erected by the bosses. The strikers and their sympathizers got an accurate account each day of key developments during the previous twenty-four hours. An analysis was made of significant moves by the bosses, the federal mediators, and Gov-

ernor Olson. The whole labor movement was alerted against
dangers that arose, and the way to cope with them was carefully explained. Although only a two-page tabloid, the daily
Organizer packed a wallop and the working class of the city
soon came to swear by it.

The paper's circulation quickly leaped to 10,000 and it soon
became self-financing. No price was set for single copies. People were simply asked to donate what they could. Salespeople
carried sealed cans with a slot in which to receive contributions. These cans were frequently stuffed with dollar bills and
as much as five dollars was paid for a single paper. People
who sold on a regular basis developed routes, leaving batches
of the paper at newsstands, beer taverns, beauty parlors, and
other establishments patronized by workers. Sales distributions
were made at factory gates, in the railway yards, wherever
workers could be reached at their jobs. People in cars stopped
by the strike headquarters to get the paper. Unions and farm
organizations throughout the state wrote to ask that copies of
The Organizer be sent to them daily.

Quick to recognize the inherent strength of the strike daily,
the capitalists tried hard to suppress it. The Citizens Alliance
began to propagandize for prosecution of those responsible for
its publication on "criminal syndicalism" charges. Nothing came
of that effort but real trouble was made in another way. When
the first issue of the daily was published, the bosses pressured
the printer into refusing to handle further editions. The paper
moved to another shop and the experience was repeated. This
happened with three successive printers. Each time the paper
was delayed several hours in publication, which caused anxious
irritation at strike headquarters. Finally Argus press took the
job and it printed the paper from then on, standing up firmly
against all pressures.

Ace Johnston, the linotype operator at Argus, commented
on this situation in an interview with *The Organizer* after the
strike: "We never knew what would happen next. We knew
we stood a good chance of having our presses smashed, the
building wrecked . . . we knew what kind of a fight it was.
But we were working with a cool-headed bunch of strike leaders, who knew their business, and we went along." Ace also
gave an example of the harassment to which they were subjected by the Citizens Alliance: "I remember one incident that
almost robbed us of a whole night's work . . . that was the
time a bunch of thugs hid at our shipping entrance, and

jumped the truck that was pulling out with an edition of the bulletin [*The Organizer*]. There was a hell of a fight, but when the smoke of battle cleared, the 574 driver and a couple of helpers had cleaned house on the finks. After that, they kept away from the Argus."

The bosses had made their quick attack on the strike daily as part of a deadly plan they were cooking up against the union. They had no intention whatever of recognizing Local 574. Actually they still hoped to smash the strike by resorting to more extreme violence against the pickets than had been employed in May. Remaining distrustful of Governor Olson's reliability in using the National Guard as a strikebreaking force, the Citizens Alliance turned its attention to strengthening the city police. Chief Johannes, who worked hand in glove with the bosses, took the lead in pushing through a big raise in the police budget in order to add more cops to the force and provide special armaments for them. This time there was no fooling around with unreliable deputies. Instead the trained cops were issued riot guns, a shotgun-type weapon using a special shell containing large scattershot that really tore up human flesh.

As a propaganda cover for the murderous plot, the *Minneapolis Journal* of July 19 printed a vicious editorial attacking the "communists" of Local 574. "But let them beware," this capitalist newspaper warned, "lest an aroused citizenry here take vigorous measures against them."

Bloody Friday

Early Thursday afternoon, July 19, 1934, Chief Michael J. Johannes issued special orders at a police lineup. As reported in the *Minneapolis Tribune,* he said: "We're going to start moving goods. Don't take a beating. You have shotguns and you know how to use them. When we are finished with this convoy there will be other goods to move."

The "convoy" to which Johannes referred was actually a carefully laid plot against the workers. That afternoon about 150 cops armed with riot guns were sent in squad cars to Jordon-Stevens Company, a wholesale grocer in the market district. There a five-ton truck was loaded with a half dozen boxes weighing a total of some 150 pounds. Banners marked "Hospital Supplies" were displayed on the truck so that reporters and photographers could depict the operation as an errand of "mercy." Special newspaper editions announcing the convoy's "success" were on the streets even before the delivery to Eitel Hospital had been completed. This camouflage was totally uncalled for because the union freely issued permits for hospital deliveries, and therein lay the plot.

In making a delivery without a union permit, the bosses hoped to weaken the strikers' morale by showing that the cops could move a truck in spite of them. They also counted on making people think that the strike was hurting the hospitals. Above all, they wanted to provoke union resistance so the cops could shoot pickets under a good propaganda cover. We refused to fall into the trap. All our cruising squads were recalled from the scene, and the delivery was allowed to go through without interference.

After describing exactly what had happened, the next issue of *The Organizer* pointed out: "The boss press, incidentally, unanimously reports the whole incident as a serious break in the strike front. This is an attempt to save something out of the failure of the plot. Happily, the *Organizer* can get the truth to the workers of Minneapolis. The picket lines are un-broken! The fight goes on!" This really irritated the bosses, who responded by engineering intensified police interference with *Organizer* salespeople.

The night before that trap was laid for the union, a special federal mediator, Reverend Francis J. Haas, had come from Washington to work with Dunnigan. Upon arrival he asked to talk with Ray Dunne and me, as the union negotiators, and we had arranged to meet with him on Thursday after-noon. Then the police action came at Jordan-Stevens that same afternoon. We immediately broke the appointment with Haas, telling him that we wouldn't meet while such a provocation was going on. After that Haas consulted Governor Olson. They joined in asking Johannes to hold up any further ac-tion for forty-eight hours — until Saturday, July 21 — so that Haas could try to negotiate a settlement of the strike.

Olson later claimed that Johannes "promised Father Haas and me that he would not convoy any trucks until Saturday evening." The police chief denied having made such a prom-ise. He admitted, however, that immediately after the Jordon-Stevens "convoy" he had met with the employers at the Radis-son Hotel. "They said they would not accept any truce," Johannes stated, "and at the same time requested me to furnish guards for the trucks." All this came to light through reports in the *Minneapolis Daily Star* of Saturday, July 21, published in the aftermath of a police riot known in the city's history as Bloody Friday. That grisly event was to win Johannes the epithet "Bloody Mike," and thereafter the working class uttered his name as a curse word.

Police guards had been demanded by the bosses to carry out their own murderous plans for "settlement" of the strike. Two steps toward that end were taken on Friday, July 20. Letters were sent to all strikers giving them three days to re-turn to work, or find themselves replaced in their jobs. At the same time preparations were made for heavily armed po-lice to convoy another truck. On this occasion there would be no pretense of a "mercy" errand to a hospital. An outright attempt to resume deliveries on a regular commercial basis was planned, and the cops were expected to shoot anyone who might interfere with the operation. The intended message to the strikers was plain enough: "Return to work or scabs will be given your jobs. If you try to stop the scabs, you can lose your life." As on the previous day, news reporters and photographers were invited to the intended scene of action. This was obviously done so that news accounts and pictures of the scene would convince every worker that the bosses meant business.

The union leadership expected another strikebreaking move to be made on Friday, most likely in the wholesale grocery area of the market. Since plenty of pickets were available and some activity would be good for their morale—things having been rather quiet—large numbers were assigned early in the morning to patrol the district. Harry DeBoer was in command of the operation. Although a considerable number of cops were also on hand, they did not appear at first to be looking for trouble. Their initial attitude is indicated by a report Harry later gave to me: "During the morning a police captain approached me on the basis that it was bad for the town to have all these pickets on Washington Avenue—with tourists going through, etc. I agreed that if the police would leave, we would leave. One car of pickets and one squad car [of cops] would remain, but no trucks were to move."

Nothing much resulted from the discussion recounted by Harry, probably because the captain soon received new orders from Johannes. Before long the police were on the prod, their change in attitude coinciding with unusual activity at Slocum-Bergren, a wholesale grocery house near Third Street and Sixth Avenue North. It appeared that an attempt was going to be made to carry out a delivery by truck. The new development was reported to strike headquarters and reinforcements were sent to the scene, bringing the picket force up to about 5,000. All the strikers were completely unarmed. We knew we couldn't challenge the riot guns, and it was our intention to conduct a peaceful mass protest against the anticipated strikebreaking move.

About this time a group of Communist Party members, led by Sam K. Davis, tried to talk Harry DeBoer into an ultraleft adventure. The incident graphically illustrated the stupidity of their "third period" line. Harry gave the pertinent facts in his report mentioned previously: "I was in charge and a committee of Stalinists . . . came to me and they proposed that we go down and take over the Court House, rather than to waste our time stopping one truck. Fortunately, I already had some knowledge of Trotskyist methods, plus I was also certain that would be a sure way of personally getting shot. So I said no."

A foot patrol of some fifty cops was on the scene, carrying riot guns as well as service revolvers and clubs. Around 2:00 P. M. they became quite tense, and within a few minutes a scab truck pulled up to the Slocum-Bergren loading dock. It was escorted by about 100 more cops in squad cars, riot guns sticking out of the car windows like quills on a porcupine. The truck had wire mesh around the cab and the license plates had been removed. A few small cartons of groceries were loaded onto it, the pickets jeering the scabs doing the rotten job. Then the fink rig pulled away from the dock and started up the street. It was followed by a picket truck, an open-bodied vehicle of the type used for dirt hauling, in which nine or ten unarmed pickets were standing.

Suddenly, without any warning whatever, the cops opened fire on the picket truck, and they shot to kill. In a matter of seconds two of the pickets lay motionless on the floor of the bullet-riddled truck. Other wounded either fell to the street, or tried to crawl out of the death trap as the shooting continued. From all quarters strikers rushed toward the truck to help them, advancing into the gunfire with the courage of lions. Many were felled by police as they stopped to pick up their injured comrades. By this time the cops had gone berserk. They were shooting in all directions, hitting most of their victims in the back as they tried to escape, and often clubbing the wounded after they fell. So wild had the firing become that a sergeant was shot by one of his own men.

The criminal nature of the police action was later attested to by a special investigating commission appointed by the governor. In its findings the commission stated: "Police took direct aim at the pickets and fired to kill. . . . Physical safety of police was at no time endangered. . . . No weapons were in the possession of the pickets in the truck. . . . At no time did pickets attack the police, and it was obvious that pickets came unprepared for such an attack."

Further evidence of the police crime was implicit in the court's findings when pickets arrested on Bloody Friday were brought to trial. All were released by the judge for lack of proof that they were guilty of any wrongdoing. To round out the picture of police sadism, *The Organizer* published a report from an outraged waitress describing Bloody Mike's dinner menu after the shooting: "soup, steak, potatoes, spinach, beans, salad, pie, cheese, coffee and a big cigar!"

While Johannes was whetting his appetite on their misery,

the pickets were withdrawing from the nightmarish scene in
the market district as best they could. In doing so they managed to bring almost all the wounded back to strike headquarters, thanks to many individual acts of heroism. Their
arrival was chronicled by Marvel Scholl in her diary. She
also pictured what it was like for the women who were staffing
the headquarters while the men were out facing the cops with
riot guns.

"Bloody Friday," she wrote, "as those of us who lived through
that awful day when death rode into the strike headquarters
know it, began as a murky, cloudy day. The very air seemed
charged with foreboding. The usual rush of business for the
auxiliary came with daylight. The kitchen opened as usual.
There was the regular amount of relief work, the *Organizer*
went to press, pickets came and went on their assignments. . . .
Yet everything was different. Perhaps the fact that the men were
gradually being weeded out of headquarters and sent down
to the market area helped create this atmosphere. . . . When
the doors of the commissary were opened for the noon meal
and only a few men appeared, we were beginning to wonder.
Mrs. Carle, who chaired the commissary committee, expressed
herself about this, saying: 'There must be something unusual
going on, Mrs. Dobbs. Kelly hasn't sent me a single cruiser
car special this morning. Bill [Gray] says that hardly any
of the night crews have come in. I'm keeping food ready,
however. I expect an awful rush when they do come in.' There
wasn't much food used that day. After the noon hour headquarters was strangely empty. It was so quiet that it was
almost eerie. . . . Even the ringing of the telephone was a
welcome diversion. And then, all too suddenly, the emptiness
gave way to overcrowding. The stillness, to the awful siren of
the ambulance. And the spotless white of the hospital quarters
to appalling red, blood red.

"When the first man was carried in [by the returning pickets],"
Marvel continued, "foaming at the mouth, gray as cement, unconscious, someone screamed. In less time that it can be told,
47 men lay on improvised cots, their bodies riddled with bul-
let wounds. Action! Water, alcohol, cotton, men and women
bathing horrid blue welts from which blood oozed. Cutting
away clothing. Lighting cigarettes for the men who lay there,
gripping their hands, biting their lips, to keep from screaming.
One of them was a red-haired boy, a messenger boy who had
been a bystander. His hand shook as he accepted his cigarette.

He smiled, whispered a weak 'thanks lady,' as he fainted. Another was Henry Ness. His shirt had been cut away, exposing his back, completely covered with blue welts. He raised himself in his delerium, fighting away the doctor who was trying to help him; he collapsed. And then the scream of the ambulances. Clear the way! Stand back! Let the cars into the garage! Nothing else enters! One by one they back in, and when they come out they are loaded with their cargo of suffering humanity. Ness and Belor in the first one. Shugren, unconscious, was lifted up . . . swiftly he was carried to the ambulance. Harry DeBoer lying on a cot. Angrily he ordered the attendants to "Take care of some of those other guys first." Harry had a slug in his leg, embedded in the bone just above the knee. Now the ambulances were being filled to their doors with all the men who were able to stand. Full to the brim, they back out, one by one, until 47 men are on their way to beds of pain and some to oblivion."

A total of sixty-seven people were wounded, over fifty of them pickets and the rest bystanders who got caught in the police fire. The overwhelming majority were shot in the back. Dr. McCrimmon reported to the union that the thirty-four men on whom he performed surgery carried 160 pieces of lead in their bodies. Those most gravely injured were Henry Ness, John Belor, and Otis Shugren. Of the three only Shugren survived. There could easily have been more fatalities, except for the promptness with which Dr. J. A. Enright and Dr. B. I. Saliterman stepped in to help Dr. McCrimmon after the tragedy. Many people came forward to volunteer blood transfusions. No less than twenty-five registered nurses made themselves available without pay for emergency calls twenty-four hours a day. The women's auxiliary set up a special committee to make daily rounds of the hospitals, assisting the wounded. People from various walks of life came to the strike headquarters with fruit, cookies, and reading material intended for the comfort and cheer of hospitalized strikers.

As part of their propaganda in preparing for Bloody Friday, the bosses had run paid ads in the daily papers, asking: "How do you like having our Minneapolis streets in the control of communists?" After the police riot *The Organizer* countered with a headline putting the real question of the hour: "How do you like having our Minneapolis streets in the control of murderers?" Addressing itself to the bosses, the union paper declared: "You thought you would shoot Local 574 into obliv-

ion. But you only succeeded in making 574 a battlecry on the
lips of every self-respecting working man and working woman
in Minneapolis. You thought you would seperate the rank
and file from their leaders. You only succeeded in cementing
the bond that holds them together in an efficient fighting army.
You thought you would alienate the labor movement from
574. You only succeeded in rallying every section of the labor
movement to our cause."

There was no exaggeration in what *The Organizer* said.
News of the shooting traveled swiftly along the working-class
grapevine, accompanied by rumors that the police were preparing to raid strike headquarters. Soon about thirty-five structural iron workers, armed with short iron bars, came to the
headquarters, ready to help defend it. Other workers followed
them, carrying implements of their trade as weapons. Hundreds
of people, representing every section of the working class,
decided to stay through the night at the headquarters, just in
case it should be raided. To show that the workers meant
business, all the hated police were chased from the surrounding
area and pickets directed traffic in that vicinity. There had
been some indication that Johannes had planned such a raid,
but that when he saw the workers' mood he had changed
his mind, concentrating instead on the fortification of city hall.

After Thursday's provocation, Local 574 had scheduled an
open-air protest meeting for the evening of July 20, to be held
on a vacant plot of ground at Seventh Street and Fourth
Avenue South. During the interim the police riot had occurred,
and when the meeting began as scheduled, over 15,000 angry
workers were present. Various AFL officials and a spokesman for the Farmers' Holiday Association joined with Local
574 leaders in addressing the rally. D. T. Boner, an officer of
the Independent Grocers Association, also spoke, calling for a
boycott of wholesale grocers in the area where the shooting
took place. The rally adopted a resolution condemning Mayor
Bainbridge and Bloody Mike for the police brutality and pledg-
ing unswerving support to Local 574.

By this time it had been made plain that Minneapolis was
witnessing a naked class battle between workers and capitalists.
Hatred of the Citizens Alliance mounted throughout the city
as it tried to justify the brutal tactics of the trucking bosses.
Attempts to put abstract subjects like "communism" and "revolution" above the concrete issues of the strike didn't wash.
Most people now felt they had to take sides on a class basis.

As for the workers of the city, they were thoroughly aroused and fighting mad. Large sections of the middle classes threw their support to the union, doing what they could to back it in the clash with the Citizens Alliance. Instead of breaking the strike, the vicious boss attack had given it new energy.

Money was donated by other unions, some of them assessing the members a day's pay in support of the strike. Several Farmer-Labor Party ward clubs in the city volunteered their services to the strike committee. The women's auxiliary recruited over fifty new members within Local 574 families, and many other women gave it backing as sympathizers. A free barber shop was set up at strike headquarters, operated by union barbers. People crowded the vicinity of the headquarters, eager to hear news bulletins and announcements over the loudspeaker. *The Organizer* reported: "Brother Sloan begs to announce that the loudspeaker at Headquarters now has a signature; it is station Five Seven Four."

On Saturday morning the massing of pickets and cruising cars at the headquarters was at least four times as great as it had been on any previous morning of the strike. Among the pickets were walking wounded from Bloody Friday who reported for duty in bandages. One of them, a war veteran, told an *Organizer* reporter: "I took it in France because I had to. Now I take it because I want to. This fight has just begun." The Yellow Cab drivers, who had been working under contract since June 4, had stayed on the job by union decision until July 20. After the shooting they spontaneously returned their cabs to the garage and reported to the union for picket duty, ready to stay at it for the duration of the strike.

Local 574 asked for a one-day strike by all transportation unions on Monday, July 23, as a protest against police violence. We explained that we weren't asking for a citywide general strike because the situation was "not ripe for such a strike." Behind this explanation lay a tactical problem having to do with Governor Olson and the AFL officialdom. Olson already had the National Guard mobilized and he was looking for an opening to intervene in our walkout. If a general protest strike were called it would give the AFL officials a pretext for involving Olson and we felt he could be expected to doublecross us as he had done in connection with the May walkout. We had, therefore, limited our request to the transportation unions, and the one-day protest action took place as scheduled, receiving strong support from the rank and file. Bus drivers even refused a request that they transport a contingent of the National Guard on that day. At the same time the laundry workers went on strike, declaring that they were acting in support of Local 574 and to fight for their own demands upon the laundry bosses.

There was also a new upsurge of support for Local 574 from among the unemployed, mainly involving people on federal "made work" projects financed by the Emergency Relief Administration (ERA). Prior to July 20, they had been registered by the hundreds through the Minneapolis Central Council of Workers (MCCW) to do picket duty for Local 574. Their spirited involvement is shown by the fact that over a dozen of those shot on Bloody Friday were MCCW members. Generally they had been picketing on days they didn't work on ERA projects, their alloted work time being limited. This changed after the shooting. On July 24 a meeting of delegates from the federal projects voted to call all ERA workers out on strike. The walkout was both to support Local 574 and to press their own demands on the federal government, which centered on trade-union rates of pay and a thirty-hour week. Over 5,000 ERA workers responded to the strike call, setting up their own strike committee which worked closely with Local 574's committee of 100.

Meantime Henry B. Ness had died less than forty-eight hours after he was wounded, leaving a widow and four young children. Marvel Scholl recorded her experience in helping Freda Ness prepare for the burial of her husband:

"This afternoon I went with Mrs. Ness and her brother-in-law to buy clothing for her and the children for the funeral. We got the little boys each a brown and white linen suit, the largest girl a nice dress and the baby a cunning little print. Also shoes and underwear. The children are utterly destitute for clothing. Their pleasure in 'store bought clothes' was pathetic. The home, scrubbed clean, is a typical example of many homes in Minneapolis that are kept on relief. There is a smell of poverty, a feeling of destitution. The very furniture seems to have taken on a discouraged attitude. The children's little pinched, white faces are expectantly eager — as though they still have hopes that there is a Santa Claus or Easter Bunny. Are these victims of capitalist greed to be the fathers and mothers of the coming generation?

"Mrs. Ness got a dress of printed silk. No mourning gowns for her. A practical dress — one that can be worn later for all occasions. 'Not a black dress, Mrs. Dobbs,' she begged. 'That is too much like all our life has been. My heart will be just as heavy under a light dress.' No black dress, Mrs. Ness. Let the wealthy drape themselves in heavy crepe. Their hearts do not remember any longer than will yours!"

Henry was buried on Tuesday, July 24, the services starting late in the day so that employed workers could attend. A family service was first held at the funeral parlor, which, ironically, was located across the street from the big garage used by the union in the May strike. After that a mass march of some 20,000 accompanied the slow-moving hearse to the strike headquarters on Eighth Street. During the march, traffic was tied up for hours—but there was not a cop in sight as the grim thousands gathered. Giving a splendid example of working-class discipline, the entire line of march remained free of disorder, as Local 574's cruising squads handled the traffic control. At the strike headquarters a black flag had been raised and a temporary stand erected in front of the building so that funeral orations could be delivered to the assembled throng. Bill Brown, who had known Henry Ness as a personal friend, tried to speak, but he broke down.

Passages from the main funeral oration, delivered by Albert Goldman, were published in *The Organizer*. He said in part: "The life of our murdered Brother typifies the lives of all workers. The social system gave him no chance. At an early age he was forced to work to earn a living and to make profits for his employer. Together with other workers, he was sent to kill and to be killed in the world war. What for? For freedom? No. For the sake of profits and imperialist markets for the bosses. Mark these words! There is only one way, one struggle in which a worker has a real interest. That is the struggle of Labor against Capital. . . . This struggle against oppression is no easy task. On the side of the bosses are the police, the army, the courts. The mayor of Minneapolis does not consider the lives of the strikers worth protecting. The only thing of importance to him is the protection of the bosses' property, the bosses' right to keep workers enslaved at low wages and in misery. . . . Brothers, Sisters, as we leave this demonstration we must bear in our hearts a fierce resolve to carry on Brother Ness's struggle. We must not fail him! We must avenge his murder. This we shall do if we struggle to win this strike, if we struggle to throw the exploiters from off our backs and to establish a new social order in which the worker may enjoy the fruits of his toil."

After Goldman had spoken the mass march was continued,

accompanying the hearse as far as Twelfth Street and First
Avenue North. More thousands of people lined the streets along
the way, most removing their hats in respect for Local 574's
martyr. Those who didn't sometimes got their hats knocked
off. By previous order of the strike committee, a large body
of Local 574 members returned to the headquarters after the
march was over to resume picketing. Other thousands, riding
in hundreds upon hundreds of automobiles, went on to the
cemetery on the north side of town. Henry was an overseas
veteran of the first world war, and the Veterans of Foreign
Wars had arranged for a squad of federal troops from Fort
Snelling to give him full military honors at the graveside.
All told over 40,000 had participated in the funeral, either
in the mass march, or in the service at strike headquarters,
or in the cortege to the cemetery. Among them were workers
from every trade and industry, organized and unorganized,
as well as many thousands of unemployed.

The massive turnout for the Ness funeral gave impetus to
another form of protest against police brutality. Within hours
after the shooting on July 20 demands had been raised that
Johannes be fired and that the City Council impeach Mayor
Bainbridge. Although we were aware that the demands could
not be realized, Local 574 helped to launch a mass campaign
around them. We did so because the pressure of such a propaganda campaign could help to make the bosses somewhat
more cautious about their use of police violence against the
strike. Being equally aware that the impeachment campaign
gave them a problem, the bosses launched their own propaganda counteroffensive. The capitalist press lauded the "brav-
ery" of the cops. Endorsements of the police action came from
the Kiwanis, the Rotary Club, the Lions, and other "civic and
commerce" organizations of the ruling class.

Petitions backing the impeachment demand were signed by
about 140,000 people. So heavy was the mass pressure that
the City Council had to agree to public hearings on a motion by a bloc of Farmer-Labor Party aldermen that Bainbridge be investigated with a view toward impeachment. At the
hearings the council chamber was packed — trade unionists as
well as agents of the ruling class turned out in force. Acrimo-
nious debate took place along sharply delineated class lines.
In the end, however, nothing was done about the demands,
an outcome that conformed with one of the basic aspects of
class struggle.

Under capitalism the main police function is to break strikes and to repress other forms of protest against the policies of the ruling class. Any civic usefulness other forms of police activity may have, like controlling traffic and summoning ambulances, is strictly incidental to the primary repressive function. Personal inclinations of individual cops do not alter this basic role of the police. All must comply with ruling-class dictates. As a result, police repression becomes one of the most naked forms through which capitalism subordinates human rights to the demands of private property. If the cops sometimes falter in their antisocial tasks, it is simply because they — like the guns they use — are subject to rust when not engaged in the deadly function for which they are primarily trained.

No police organization is exactly the same day in and day out. Two essential factors determine its character at a given moment: the social climate in which the cops have been operating and the turnover of personnel within the force. An unseasoned cop may tend to be somewhat considerate of others in the performance of duty, especially while class relations are relatively peaceful. Even in such calm times, however, the necessary accommodation must be made to capitalist demands, including readiness to shoot anyone who tampers with private property. Otherwise the aspiring cop, if he is not kicked out of the force, will have little chance of rising beyond a beat in the sticks. By gradually weeding out misfits along these general lines, a police department can keep itself abreast of requirements during a more or less stable period in class relations.

Such had been the case with the Minneapolis cops, whose strikebreaking experiences had long been limited to occasional attacks on weak craft unions that were poorly led. Then in 1934 a sharp turn occurred in the class struggle, and they were found to be less than competent in carrying out the harsh new tasks imposed upon them by the bosses. To play the required role in the changed alignment of class forces, the department had to be drastically shaken up, and it was. When Johannes first issued riot guns to the cops a few had declined to take them, and they were immediately suspended from the force. Another handful drew suspensions when they took the guns but refused to use them. Two or three went so far as to join in the shooting, and then probably appalled by the resultant carnage, turned in their guns and badges. Among those suspended was a captain of police, John Hart. Through this general shakeup the Minneapolis police force had become transformed into a body of uniformed killers who were ready to shoot strikers upon command.

In the meantime Local 574's pickets were reacting to the police assault in full keeping with their magnificent fighting spirit. After the shooting, many who had escaped injury dropped from sight briefly, only to return soon armed with various kinds of weapons. They now had shotguns, deer rifles, revolvers, hunting knives, and various types of souvenirs from World War I, which the veterans among them had brought back from France. Having bested the cops club-against-club in May, the strikers were now prepared to face them gun-against-gun. Although their cause was just and their courage admirable, it would have been a grave tactical mistake to attempt to go through with such an undertaking.

The situation was now qualitatively different from what it had been during the earlier battle with clubs. Despite the fact that a club can kill, it is not usually classified as a deadly weapon. By virtue of that fact, self-defense of the kind used in May could be sustained tactically for several reasons: it was carried out by a massive body of pickets who had widespread sympathy within the city as a whole; for reasons described previously, Governor Olson found it difficult to use the state militia against the union; and due to the insular nature of the conflict and the local politics involved, President Roosevelt had little inclination and no ready pretext to intervene with federal troops. Consequently the fighting in May remained confined to a showdown between the pickets and the local cops.

As matters stood after Bloody Friday, however, the situation was entirely different. Guns and knives are known as lethal weapons. Being so deadly, their use in self-defense against the gun-toting cops could have been twisted around by capitalist propaganda into the appearance of an "insurrectionary offensive" by the strikers. The bosses would have screamed bloody murder, claiming proof of their contention that our aim was not to build a union but to make a revolution. At the first armed skirmish between strikers and police a clamor would have been raised for Olson and Roosevelt to send troops against the union. Olson would have been quick to do so, feeling that he now had a valid political excuse for putting an end to the whole knotty problem. In case Olson didn't act effectively, Roosevelt would have felt free to send federal troops because he could claim that he was suppressing an "insurrection."

Local 574, against which such military repression would have been directed, was engaged in an isolated local action. Nationally, our struggle was paralleled only by two other similarly isolated conflicts involving auto workers in Toledo and longshoremen in San Francisco. The nation's working class in general was only beginning to move toward unionization and its main detachments were not yet ready for combat. In these circumstances, Local 574 could have mustered very little real support outside Minneapolis itself. Hence, it could not have withstood the heavy military pressure; the strike would have been broken and the union crushed.

This was a situation in which the central strike leadership had to act swiftly and decisively. Otherwise impulsive pickets, looking for a showdown with the cops, could have done irreparable damage to the union's cause while the policy question was being debated. The pickets had to be disarmed forthwith, and the central leaders had to do it on their own responsibility. Ray Dunne and I pitched in to help Kelly Postal confiscate the weapons from each cruising squad as it was sent out on a picketing mission.

It wasn't easy, nor was it pleasant. For my part, I still consider it the hardest thing I ever did in my life. Understandably, we got some stiff arguments and some uncomplimentary descriptions of our attitude. In the end, however, the weapons were handed over, thanks to the union's well-established disciplinary norms and to the leadership authority we had earned. Once again, Local 574's incomparable soldiers went out barehanded to face cops with riot guns.

Our action was promptly reported to a meeting of the strike committee, and the reasons were given for the policy we had followed. After considerable debate the committee approved the course taken, issuing picketing orders accordingly. The orders, which were published in *The Organizer*, contained a deliberately obscure formulation: "All pickets are instructed to continue tactics of peaceful picketing as hitherto. They are, however, to defend themselves against any attacks." Since we hadn't troubled to let the cops know whether or not the pickets were armed, they weren't sure what permission to "defend themselves" meant, and being aware of the strikers' anger, the cops weren't in a hurry to find out.

How well the pickets could handle themselves in this hazardous situation would depend largely on the competence and authority of their captains. In this regard we had a problem because of the injury sustained on Bloody Friday by Harry

DeBoer, who had been among those advancing into the gunfire to rescue wounded pickets. Harry would have to be replaced
in his role as one of the principal field commanders of picketing operations. With a very complex tactical situation now
facing us, other changes in the command structure also had
to be made. Kelly Postal, who had been serving as chief picket
dispatcher, was reassigned to a central field command. Ray
Rainbolt and Jack Maloney were given similar assignments
in keeping with needs of the tactical methods we would now
use. Henry Schultz, a railway brakeman who had volunteered
to help Local 574, was assigned by the strike committee to
the dispatcher's function, and as Kelly had done, he acted
in consultation with Ray Dunne and me.

Our task was to checkmate the strategy used by Johannes
after the shooting. He was beginning to feel his way gingerly
into an attempt to resume trucking operations under police
escort. As a starter he used about forty squad cars, loaded
with cops carrying riot guns, to convoy a single truck. The
operation was flanked by an even larger detachment of Local
574's cruising picket squads. Our pickets didn't try to stop
the truck; they just made it plain that lots of cops were needed
to move it. Johannes next tried to increase the number of convoys undertaken, reducing the size of the police escort used in
each case. His plan was obviously to proceed along this line
until enough trucks were moving at one time to crack the
strikers' morale and whittle away the union's strength through
desertions.

As Johannes reduced the size of the police escorts, we countered by increasing the number of union cruising squads flanking each convoy. This change in the relation of forces with
respect to each single convoy implied the danger of union
action to halt the scab trucks, and the cops still didn't know
whether or not the pickets were armed. Johannes thus felt compelled to beef up the escort for the convoys, which made it
necessary to reduce them in number. As a result of this tug
of war the bosses found themselves unable to resume trucking
operations to any significant degree. The cops were again
failing in their mission. Even cold-blooded murder hadn't been
able to stop Local 574.

RALPH R. GAMBLE. PRES.   FRANK C. REED. VICE-PRES.   ALBERT J. MEYERS. VICE-PRES.   ROBERT G. GAMBLE. SEC. & TREAS.

Northwest Fruit & Produce Co.

INCORPORATED. CAPITAL STOCK. $100,000

WHOLESALE FRUITS, VEGETABLES, PRODUCE

TELEPHONE
ATLANTIC 5487

218-220-222 SIXTH STREET NORTH
MINNEAPOLIS, MINNESOTA

REFERENCES:
PRODUCE STATE BANK
ANY COMMERCIAL AGENCY

July 20, 1934

William Schoener

Dear Sir:

We wish to inform you that if you care to return to work, you may do so by reporting for duty on or before Monday July 23. After that date any other qualified applicants will be considered for employment on a permanent basis.

Kindly govern yourself accordingly and get in touch with us if this is not thoroughly understood.

We have lived up to the Labor Board's Order which settled the strike in May. We believe that you have been misled into going out "on strike" against us. This may cause you to lose rights granted by that Order.

Your co-operation is desired, but if it is not obtained we will be obliged to carry on without you.

Yours very truly,

NORTHWEST FRUIT & PRODUCE CO.

This letter, originally sent by Northwest Fruit Company to striking employee William Schoener, is from the files of Local 574. It bears the date of Bloody Friday, July 20, 1934.

"Suddenly, without any warning whatever, the cops opened
fire on the picket truck (above), and they shot to kill. In a
matter of seconds two of the pickets lay motionless on the
floor of the bullet-riddled truck (below)."

Local 574 strikers place memorial wreath and plaque for Henry Ness above entrance to strike headquarters, 215 South Eighth Street. Quoted on the plaque are Ness's last words: "Tell the boys not to fail me now."

A procession of Local 574's "cruising pickets" during massive funeral ceremony held for Henry Ness, Tuesday, July 24, 1934.

'Don't Fail Me Now Boys!' — Last Words of Henry B. Ness
Shot in the Back In Cold
Blood by Order of Michael Johannes the Murderer. Died July 21st, 1934

DAILY STRIKE BULLETIN

**UNITED
LABOR
ACTION**

THE ORGANIZER
574
TWO TWENTY-FIVE   SOUTH THIRD STREET

**SMASH THE
CITIZENS
ALLIANCE**

Volume 1, No. 10   MINNEAPOLIS, MINNESOTA, MONDAY, JULY 23, 1934   Price

The Fight Has Just Begun

Laundry Men to Strike Tuesday; Solid with 574

Drop Parley With Bosses; Condemn Johannes

The First Martyr of 574

HENRY NESS

Henry B. Ness, martyr of labor's struggle, was born March 18, 1894, in Eau Claire, Wisconsin. He served overseas in the World War. He is survived by Mrs. Freda Ness and four children: Olive, age 9; Henry, Jr., age 7; William, age 5; John, age 1½, living at 2812 Tenth Ave. South.

For 16 years Brother Ness was an active and loyal trade unionist, for the last few years in the General Drivers Union, Local 574. His fellow Unionists respected his opinions and his courage, and found his genial disposition a source of constant pleasure.

Ordered to the picket line in the wholesale grocery district Friday morning, he went forth with a determination to fight to the end for the rights of labor. When the police opened fire on the peaceful picketers, Brother Ness received a charge of shot full in the chest. As he turned to seek shelter, a cowardly enemy buried another charge in his back. Thirty-eight slugs in all parts of his body were more than doctors could fight against. Union brothers gave liberally of their blood to save him but the sacrifices did not avail.

The Testament of Henry Ness

All Out to the Funeral!

Bosses' Threats Fail to Worry 574's Picketers

More Men Out Than Ever; Town Still Tied Up

Front page of the July 23 Organizer following the death of union member Henry Ness.

Military Strikebreaking

With the conflict between Local 574 and the Citizens Alliance
at a point of extreme tension, Governor Olson decided to take
a direct hand in the dispute. Military forces for the purpose
had already been mobilized. At the outset of the strike, part
of the National Guard had been called up; the troops were
billeted at the State Fair Grounds; and a military headquarters
was set up at the armory on Sixth Street and Fourth Avenue
South. So far the guard had been used only for a brief time
on Bloody Friday.

In the aftermath of the police assault on the pickets that
day, troops had been rushed to the scene of the shooting and
about an hour later they had been withdrawn to their quarters.
At the same time, Olson had sent a reported 4,000 additional
guardsmen into the city and had ordered another 2,000 to
ready themselves for strike duty. The *Minneapolis Daily Star*
of July 21, 1934, quoted him as saying that if he found it
necessary to assume military control, "I will make the city of
Minneapolis as quiet as a Sunday school."

Local 574 responded to the governor's threat through a
stinging editorial in *The Organizer*. The union paper noted
that martial law meant the existance of a state of war that
could not be dealt with by the ordinary police. It said that
there was a war going on in Minneapolis, and described the
conflict as one of poverty against wealth, of labor against
capital. "We never asked for protection from the guard," the
editorial continued. "We have no 'property' to protect. The
employers have. It is their properties and their profits extorted
from our labor that they want protected. It is their scabs and
their scab trucks, sent out to rob us of our bread, that they

want protected. We never called for the troops. The employers did. We call for their withdrawal. . . . We don't need the guard to stop scab trucks. But the employers need it to convoy them through. . . . Guardsmen's bayonets, tear gas guns or trench helmets cannot move trucks. . . . You need truck drivers and helpers and platform men and inside men to move trucks. And they are all in the ranks of 574. And that's where they are going to stay. And under its banner they are going to win."

Olson had good reason to know that Local 574's reaction to his threat of military intervention was not mere bluster. Yet he wanted desperately to end the walkout, feeling that it endangered him politically at a time when he would soon be coming up for reelection. He was incapable of staking his political fate on uncompromising loyality to the working class. His policy was to build a personal political career on the assurance that he could be trusted to follow capitalist ground rules in exercising governmental authority. At the same time he had to avoid estrangement of Farmer-Labor Party members whose support was vital to his political future. This meant that in attempting to force through a settlement of the dispute he could not afford to cast himself openly in the role of strikebreaker.

In an effort to solve the problem, the governor devised a ploy involving the collaboration of Haas and Dunnigan, the federal mediators. They were to probe the union and employer positions to see if the threat of martial law had given rise to any new prospects for a compromise. Haas and Dunnigan would then publicly propose the terms for what they considered a "fair" settlement of the strike. Olson would back their proposal, stressing that it was a federal recommendation, thereby implying support from the Roosevelt administration. At the same time, the governor would threaten to declare martial law as a means of forcing a settlement on the Haas-Dunnigan terms. If the employers' committee rejected the proposed settlement, he would encourage individual bosses to accept it and operate their trucks under military protection.

Olson hoped for enough individual responses along these lines to break the solid front maintained by the Citizens Alliance. It followed that rejection of the Haas-Dunnigan proposal by Local 574 would lead directly to military strikebreaking. The governor would count on getting away with this politically through propaganda about a "fair" settlement. He would get additional support from conservative AFL officials.

Local 574 got the first inkling of the scheme when Haas and Dunnigan began an exchange of memoranda with the union and the bosses. On the question of union recognition, the mediators proposed a Labor Board election for employees to choose "representatives," omitting any mention of Local 574, The union demanded that its name be on the ballot and that in every company where it won a majority it should represent all employees. The bosses rejected the union demand, insisting on the abstract reference to "representatives." However, they did show signs of weakening with reference to the scope of union representation.

Haas and Dunnigan proposed the inclusion of inside workers at the twenty-two market firms, defining them as employees other than drivers, office workers, and salesmen. For the remaining firms, they proposed recognition only for drivers, helpers, and platform workers directly engaged in loading and unloading trucks. The bosses hinted that they might accept this overall definition.

Local 574 was amenable to the definition of inside workers in the case of the twenty-two market firms, which included fruit, produce, packers, wholesale grocers, and fish houses. We demanded, however, the right to represent more than drivers, helpers, and platform workers at nonmarket firms, pressing for the inclusion of warehouse and shipping department employees.

On the eve of the strike the union had called for minimum hourly rates of 55¢ for drivers and 45¢ for helpers, platform men, and inside workers. The mediators wanted these figures shaved down to 52 1/2¢ and 42 1/2¢ for the respective categories. Insisting that the matter would have to be negotiated or arbitrated, the bosses refused to commit themselves to any wage scale at all. They also wanted to keep their scabs on the payroll and fire any strikers "found guilty of violence."

PROPOSED SETTLEMENT

After this exchange of views on key issues in the strike, Haas and Dunnigan proceeded to announce publicly their proposed terms for a "fair settlement." Their proposal was issued on July 25, the day after the Ness funeral. It stipulated that all strikers were to be reinstated without discrimination. A Labor Board election was to be held within three days after the strike ended. In the twenty-two market firms, all employees, except salesmen and office workers, would be eligible to vote and they were to vote as a group. Outside the market, only drivers, helpers, and platform workers would be eligible to vote, doing so on a firm-by-firm basis. The balloting would be on the question of whether or not the employees wished to be represented by Local 574. A majority vote would entitle the union to bargain for all workers. Immediately after the election there was to be negotiation and arbitration of wages and other disputed matters. The wage award was to be no less than 52 1/2¢ per hour for drivers and 42 1/2¢ for inside workers, helpers, and platform men.

Announcement of the Haas-Dunnigan proposal for settlement of the strike was immediately followed by Olson's public endorsement of its terms. The governor gave the union and the bosses twenty-four hours to act on the proposal. If either side rejected it, he declared, troops would be used to put an end to the dispute on the basis stipulated by the federal mediators. On the evening of July 25 the strike committee of 100 met to consider Olson's ultimatum. The central leaders had no difficulty in getting across to these seasoned fighters that a deadly trap was being laid for the union. It was clear that union rejection of the Haas-Dunnigan terms would subject us to direct military attack under adverse propaganda conditions. Therefore, we had to examine the situation in a cool-headed way, carefully thinking out the analysis to be presented to the union membership.

While we would have to make certain concessions in accepting the manifestly unfair settlement, nothing basic would be sacrificed. On the plus side, it provided some gain in wages over the scales the bosses had paid before the strike. We would be breaking through on the inside worker issue in the market where most of these union members were concentrated. Although warehouse and shipping-room employees organized elsewhere were not specifically included in the terms, a victorious union could force de facto recognition of its right to represent them. This expectation was reinforced by the provision enabling us to win direct recognition of the union through a Labor Board election. In fact it was precisely the union-recognition clause which made likely a rejection by the employers of the Haas-Dunnigan proposal. From this followed the probability that our acceptance of the proposal would not end the strike. It was agreed in the strike committee that an analysis along these lines should be presented to the union membership.

The committee held its meeting at the Local 574 hall on South Third Street. While we were in session a report came that the

police were raiding the strike headquarters. Everybody rushed there to help fight off the cops, only to find that it was
a false alarm. Rumors of an impending raid persisted, however,
so workers from Emergency Relief Administration projects
guarded the strike headquarters, while all Local 574 members
met at Eagles Hall on the morning of July 26. The appraisal
agreed upon the night before was presented to the meeting in the
name of the strike committee. A long discussion followed in
which various aspects of the situation were further clarified,
more or less to everyone's satisfaction. A vote was then taken
and the union accepted the mediators' terms.

Olson had set noon of that day as the deadline for an answer
from the union and the bosses. Although we came to an official decision earlier than that, we kept our silence for the time
being. We expected the bosses to hold up announcement of
their action, waiting hopefully to see if the union rejected the
proposal. If so, they would most likely have prepared a propaganda blast against us based on such an assumption. We
decided to trip them up by withholding news of our decision
until the last moment.

Although the packed hall was uncomfortably hot on that
summer morning, the windows were kept closed and the doors
locked. That prevented newspaper snoops from getting in and
informers from sneaking out. Being aware of the reasons for
this policy, the membership cheerfully stood the discomfort.
⌈Then at exactly twelve o'clock Bill Brown notified Governor
Olson that Local 574 had accepted the Haas-Dunnigan proposal.⌉

We had caught the bosses flatfooted. After some delay they
announced that the proposal was "accepted with reservations."
As *The Organizer* commented, this simply meant that they
turned it down with fancy language. The onus was now plainly
on them for continuance of the strike and they had been put
in a bad propaganda light. Trying to extricate themselves as
best they could, the bosses told Haas and Dunnigan: "We cannot deal with this Communist leadership." To Olson they put
an arrogant question: "We as citizens of Minneapolis demand
to know whether you will support local authorities with military aid?"

Local 574 also had some questions to ask. "What would have
happened," it inquired through an *Organizer* editorial, "if the
bosses had accepted a Haas plan and we had turned it down?
Not a bandit or yegg, not a pious hypocrite or snivelling

laborsweater, not a stockholder or stockjobber in town but would have yelled for our blood. And what would the Federal representative have done? What will he do now? It will be interesting to see what, if anything, the Rev. Haas has to say about the bosses who turned down the olive branch he flew with from Washington. Of course, the Rev. Haas's speech or silence will not determine the issue. The spirits of the strikers are higher than ever. Neither conciliators nor negotiators nor dictators can dampen them. We will not return to work for a pittance. . . . We will go back to work but with decent wages, decent conditions, and a Union, Local 574, to protect us. . . . Despite death and the devil, despite the whole unholy alliance which is pitted against us: the strike goes on. Peaceful picketing continues. The banner still waves on which is inscribed our slogan: No trucks shall be moved! By nobody!"

On the afternoon of July 26 Governor Olson proclaimed that a "state of insurrection" existed in Minneapolis and put the city under martial law. Some 4,000 guardsmen were soon deployed in the business areas. All picketing was forbidden, and Local 574 was denied the right to conduct open-air meetings at strike headquarters. Orders were also issued that no trucks could move without a military permit.

Olson had now come to the final stage of the ploy he had cooked up in collaboration with Haas and Dunnigan; namely, the forcing of a strike settlement through martial law. Local 574 had refused to make this easy for him, which would have been the case if it had rejected the mediators' proposal and thus laid itself open to attack. Instead the governor had to pretend to square off against the bosses who were defying him. Far from being in a position to end the conflict, he had only become more dangerously involved in it and in the process he had dug himself into a new political hole.

Olson's first reflex act in this troublesome situation was to lash out at Local 574 by allowing the military to become involved in a new red-baiting attack on the union. The Trotskyist leaders Jim Cannon and Max Shachtman had been arrested by the city police on the evening of July 25. Their hotel rooms were searched without a warrant, and scare headlines were run in the capitalist press about "evidence" uncovered that they were leaders of the Communist League. After being kept in jail about forty-eight hours, they were finally brought into court on "vagrancy" charges. Instead of putting them on trial, the judge turned them over to the military, martial law having

been declared by that time. They were taken to military headquarters, held there for several hours, and then released with
a proviso that they leave town forthwith.

To solve this problem they simply went to the next-door city
of St. Paul. Local 574 vigorously protested the frame-up of
Jim and Max, the strike committee being aware of their efforts
in support of the union and appreciative of the contributions
they were making. Olson then backed off, allowing them to
return to Minneapolis a couple of days later. Soon afterward
it became necessary for Max to go back to New York, and for
the duration of the strike Herbert Solow assumed the chief editorial responsibility for *The Organizer*.

Meanwhile, military permits were being issued to truck operators who signed the Haas-Dunnigan proposal. As is usually
the case in the trucking industry, there was a rush of small-
fry operators to sign up for permits. They did so without
hesitation because they had no intention of paying the specified
wages. However, none of the big trucking firms broke loose
from Citizens Alliance control, as Olson had hoped they would.
They merely took advantage of his ruling that special permits
would be issued for goods moving in "interstate commerce."
Before long the military was also allowing unrestricted delivery of wholesale groceries and various other commodities.
Pickets who complained to guard patrols about the policy
were often taken into military custody, usually to be held for
a few hours for purposes of intimidation. Permits were issued
to firms directly involved in the walkout, and this was used
by them as a basis for warning striking employees to return
to work or forfeit their jobs. The situation had developed into
a piecemeal process of military strikebreaking.

Olson next tried to coax the Citizens Alliance into allowing
him some kind of a concession as a face-saving cover for his
blows against Local 574. He made the pitch through a statement published in the *Minneapolis Tribune* of July 31. Military
protection for full-scale operation was offered to the struck firms
if they would do two things: pay the wage scale recommended
by Haas and Dunnigan, and reinstate striking employees who
wished to return to work. Assurance was given that this would
"not in any way involve a committal by the employers to the
entire proposal" submitted by the mediators. "It will enable
Father Haas and Commissioner Dunnigan to continue their
conciliatory efforts," the governor argued, "and it will substan-
tially aid the National Guard in keeping peace in the city."

The scheme was in reality designed to bypass the issue of union recognition. But another effect of this plan would be to promote desertions from the union's ranks by offering a wage increase, thus making it easier for the military to suppress a weakened union. Sensing that they had Olson on the run, the bosses flatly rejected his proposition. "Any settlement as so far suggested," they said in the press, "would be a surrender to a group of communist leaders who do not represent our employees."

Local 574 angrily denounced the governor's whole policy. It declared in an *Organizer* editorial: "The government officials, who roar like lions when speaking to workers, coo like suckling doves when speaking to the bosses." A delegation from the Central Labor Union, the Building Trades Council, and Local 574 met with Olson to protest the use of militia as a front for scabbing. The governor was pointedly told by Carl Skoglund, speaking for local 574, that the bosses could have been forced to accept the Haas-Dunnigan proposal, if martial law had not been declared. Carl demanded that all military permits be revoked for forty-eight hours and that future permits be granted only to employers who agreed to comply with all conditions that the mediators had recommended and the union had accepted. It was also insisted that the union have representatives on the committee issuing the permits. Either halt all trucks for forty-eight hours, Olson was told, or Local 574 will stop them. He refused to offer the cooperation requested by the union.

Paraphrasing a famous remark of General Grant's during the Civil War, *The Organizer* proclaimed: "We will fight it out on the picket line if it takes all summer." A mass rally, attended by over 25,000 workers, was held at the Parade Grounds on the evening of July 31. Bill Brown gave one of the best fighting talks he ever made. "The Farmer-Labor administration," he scornfully declared, "is the best strikebreaking force our union has ever gone up against." All supporters of Local 574 were asked to report to the strike headquarters at four A.M. the following morning, Wednesday, August 1, to resume mass picketing in defiance of the militia. If the troops fired upon us, the union would be in grave danger of defeat, but there was better than an even chance they wouldn't do so because Olson couldn't afford it politically. In any case, we had to take the risk or the strike would be broken.

After the rally, Ray and Grant Dunne and I went to strike

headquarters to help the night crew prepare things for the next day's action. Later on we curled up for a little sleep on the cushions of picket cars parked in the lot behind the garage. Toward four A.M. the night crew shook us awake and reported that the National Guard was encircling the entire block around the headquarters. Over 1,000 troops had advanced upon us under the command of Colonel Elmer McDevitt. They were spearheaded by a heavily armed shock battalion of some 300, and supported by a company of machine gunners. By the time the three of us got to the front of the building, we found the street outside packed with guardsmen who had several machine guns trained on the headquarters entrance. After a pause McDevitt came toward us, escorted by a detachment of soldiers whose bayonets glistened in the rays of the rising sun.

Not being fools, we offered no resistance. However, we had something of a reputation as fighters, and the military hadn't been sure how we would react to the attack. This was manifested by the colonel's obvious relief once he found himself inside the building and apparently safe. Although it wasn't all that hot so early in the morning, he took off his helmet and wiped the sweat from his balding head.

"Who's in charge here?", McDevitt asked.

"I am," Ray Dunne replied, always being quick to step forward in a crisis.

"What's your name?"

"Ray Dunne."

"You're under arrest," the colonel declared, ordering a guard detail to take him away.

McDevitt then took a list from his pocket and showed it to Henry Schultz, the night picket dispatcher, asking if any others on it besides Ray were present. The list contained the names of the top strike leaders and a couple of Communist Party hacks, who had been added for propaganda dressing although they had nothing whatever to do with leading the strike. Bill Brown and Miles Dunne were not present, but they were picked up before they could be warned that Olson had ordered their arrest. Carl Skoglund escaped being hauled in because he was out of town trying to raise money in support of the strike. Ray, Miles, and Bill, along with other unionists arrested later in the day for picketing, were taken to an improvised stockade at the State Fair Grounds.

While Schultz was checking the list and telling the colonel

that nobody else on it was present, he gave a discreet sign
to Grant and me. His meaning was obvious. We were wanted
and should get the hell out of there in a hurry. It was unwise to go out the front way because newspaper reporters
were out there, and their attitude upon seeing us would surely
arouse the curiosity of the military. So we left through the
rear door, passing word among the pickets on the way to
reassemble at 614 First Avenue North, the AFL headquarters.

When we got to the military lines we were stopped by a
lieutenant who said we must go out the front way. We feigned
indignation, claiming that "a guy up front with eagles on his
shoulders" had told us to leave the way we were going. The
lieutenant said he had orders to the contrary. At that we sat
down on the curb, allowing that we wouldn't move until the
army figured out who was in charge and what they wanted
people to do. The ruse worked. A runner was sent to report
the situation to McDevitt, and he sent back orders to let us
through the lines.

Henry Schultz was endowed with a stubborn streak, which
was just what the doctor ordered in that kind of a situation.
He argued that the militia had interrupted our morning meal
and finally got permission for the pickets to eat breakfast
before they left the premises. In this way word was gotten
to everyone to go to "614." Henry also talked the colonel into
letting him move part of the commissary equipment to the
AFL headquarters. In addition he insisted on a written in-
ventory of union property seized by the National Guard. This
included cars belonging to individual strikers found in the
parking lot behind the garage. The main haul, however, was
the weapons that had been taken from the pickets in the aftermath of Bloody Friday. These had been put away under lock
and key, but now the guard command took them out of storage
and put them on display so that the newspaper reporters and
photographers could build up a phony propaganda smear
against the union. About a half-dozen wounded from Bloody
Friday were still on cots in the union hospital. They were
hauled away to a military institution, and Dr. Enright, who
was caring for them, was put under arrest.

By the time Grant and I reached the AFL headquarters,
a considerable picket force had already assembled there. A
meeting of the available picket captains was quickly called
to shape plans for stopping scab trucks in defiance of Olson's
martial law. Everything would depend upon their individual

resourcefulness in the hit-and-run actions we had to conduct. They were all seasoned hands by this time, able young secondary leaders ready to step into the gap created by the governor's attack on the top union leaders. Before the day was over they proved that they had the necessary ability to do what was needed.

Since the kind of fight we intended to wage would probably bring further military raids on any suspected center of picket concentration, we decided to decentralize operations. A series of control points was set up around the town, mainly in friendly filling stations, which cruising squads could enter and leave without attracting attention. Pay phones in the stations and couriers scouting the neighborhoods were used to report scab trucks to picket dispatchers. Cruising squads were then sent to the reported locations to do the necessary and get away in a hurry. Trucks operating with military permits were soon being put out of commission throughout the city. Within a few hours over 500 calls for help were reported to have come into the military headquarters. Troops in squad cars responded to the calls usually to find scabs who had been worked over, but no pickets. Long lists of attacks on scab trucks were reported in the evening papers.

While all this was going on, the National Guard raided the AFL headquarters, ordering everybody out of the building to the dismay of the business agents who couldn't believe that Olson would do such a thing. The troops also invaded the Cooks and Waiters Union hall located at another address, where our pickets had been using the telephones. In addition they occupied the regular Local 574 hall on South Third Street. Despite everything the military tried to do, however, the supposedly headless strike was full of life. The pickets were battling furiously and they were doing it skillfully. By the end of the day only thirty-eight of them had been arrested, a small number considering the scope of the union action and the results that were being obtained.

Grant Dunne and I stayed at the AFL headquarters until we heard Pat Corcoran, the business agent for the Milk Drivers, yell, "They can't do that!" He was protesting the intrusion of guardsmen with bayoneted rifles. We decided it was no place for us to remain, and once again we managed to slip through the military dragnet. After that it was touch and go for us as we tried to keep in circulation with the radio stations broadcasting our descriptions. The hunt was so intense that the militia searched the homes of all twelve families in the apartment building where Grant lived.

Finally we got word that Robley D. Cramer, editor of the AFL *Labor Review,* had been making urgent requests for us to call him. Grant made the call, and Cramer quickly put Olson on the phone. The governor promised us immunity from arrest if we would meet with him at the *Labor Review* offices in the Sexton Building, and we agreed to do so. When we got there we found a room full of AFL business agents. They told us that the governor was in another office meeting privately with a committee from Local 574.

We learned later that after the raid on the AFL headquarters Olson had sent out a request to meet a "truly representative" rank-and-file committee from Local 574. What he got was a committee of Kelly Postal, Ray Rainbolt and Jack Maloney, three of the union's outstanding picket commanders. When they got to the Sexton Building they showed their contempt for the business agents assembled there by refusing to talk in their presence. Olson had then gone into session with them privately, saying that he wanted to negotiate a "fair" settlement of the strike. They told him they had no power to negotiate and had come simply to present certain demands. These were: release our leaders from arrest; return our strike headquarters to us; and get your troops off the streets so we can stop the scab trucking operations without further interference from them. It was with the "negotiations" thus standing on dead center that the governor had decided to send for Grant and me. He had done so after Haas made a fruitless attempt to talk with Ray and Miles Dunne and Bill Brown in the stockade. They said they wouldn't negotiate "within the confines of a military concentration camp."

When Grant and I walked into the room where Olson and our committee were in session, he seemed glad to see us. We, in turn, were happy to find such strong union representatives there. The governor was told there could be no negotiations until he agreed to release Ray, Miles, and Bill from the stockade. He said he would, and a few hours later the three were set free. The order for Carl Skoglund's arrest was also rescinded. We then demanded an explanation for the raid on the strike headquarters. Olson claimed it was because we had held a mass meeting the night before without a military permit. We told him that we did have a permit and could produce it. At this point he asked Grant and me to accompany him to the

military headquarters so that the matter could be taken up
with General Walsh. We did so, first reaching Al Goldman
by telephone and arranging for him as our attorney to meet
us there with the permit. Colonel McDevitt was also present
in the session with Walsh. He tried to argue against turning
our headquarters back to us on the ground that it would hurt
the morale of his troops.

We had Olson in a bind, however, because the permit for our
July 31 protest rally plainly read "Sound equipment and hold
a mass meeting." Stripped of the pretext he had used for the
raid, he ordered that the union premises be vacated by the
military. Around eleven P. M. on the same day that the strike
headquarters had been taken over, a guard officer formally
returned it to us. Henry Schultz was assigned to see that nothing had been damaged or stolen. Before signing a receipt
for the return of our building and equipment, Henry demanded
an exact check to see that none of the weapons that the guard
had seized were missing. He did so on the premise — sacred to
capitalism — that they were the private property of individual
strikers.

The day's events had obviously stemmed from another
"master plan" devised by the governor, the general nature of
which can readily be deduced. Using the excuse of an alleged
violation of martial law, he had hoped to put the union in an
untenable position. He thought he could seize the strike headquarters and put the blame on the Local 574 leaders on the
grounds that they were defying military authority. Such charges
would át the same time be used to justify locking us up in the
stockade, thereby removing the "communist" issue on which
the bosses based their refusal to deal with Local 574. With the
union thus beheaded, he would call for a rank-and-file committee to negotiate a settlement of the strike.

The governor apparently thought he had several things going
for him that would enable the plan to succeed. These included
his own cleverness and powers of persuasion; signs among
trucking bosses of resistance to Citizens Alliance control; his
personal prestige within the labor movement; and the help of
conservative AFL officials. The scheme may have looked good
on paper, but when the smoke cleared at the end of the day,
Olson found that he had only gotten into worse political difficulty.

Hitting back at the governor on his political flank, *The
Organizer* went after him hammer and tongs. The strike daily

had managed to come out almost on schedule despite military harassment of the union. Its editorial line in reply to Olson's attack was decided through a rather hectic process of consultation among available leaders. Al Goldman arrived at "614" while Grant and I were there, and we agreed that the paper should call for a general protest strike. Jim Cannon was then reached by telephone, and his views squared with ours. While Al prepared rough notes for an editorial, Grant and I jotted down an outline sketch of the tactical situation. Marvel Scholl was then assigned to deliver this raw material to Herbert Solow who was editing the paper. He was at Argus, where we always got maximum cooperation, but there was a possibility of military interference there. On the assumption that it might happen, arrangements were made to print the paper in St. Paul, if necessary. Toward that end, extra page proofs were pulled as the paper was set and Marvel tucked them away in her purse.

After the first 500 copies of the paper came off the press, Marvel and her picket escort took the bundles to "614," the strike headquarters not yet having been returned to us. By that time military occupation of the AFL building had ended, and Local 574 was again operating a commissary in it. The pickets on hand there set up a rousing cheer when the bundles were opened to reveal their little two-page champion. Its headlines read: "Answer Military Tyranny by a General Protest Strike!"—"Olson and State Troops Have Shown Their Colors!—Union Men Show Yours!"—"Our Headquarters Have Been Raided!—"Our Leaders Jailed!"—"574 Fights On!"

In the changed situation a reversal had occurred on the tactical aspects of the general-strike question. A broad protest action could not now be misused by conservative AFL officials as a way of promoting Olson's leadership influence to the detriment of the strike. The protest would this time be aimed squarely at the governor who was acting as an open strikebreaker. Under these conditions our call for a general strike would be entirely to Local 574's advantage. It would stimulate rank-and-file pressure on the AFL business agents to support us against Olson's attack.

We knew that union militants throughout the city were seething with anger about the military raids. The Farmer-Labor Party club at the University of Minnesota sent the governor a wire stating, "This is to notify you that you have been expelled as honorary chairman of our organization." In fact

the swift manifestation of such sentiments helped to pressure
Olson into releasing the Local 574 leaders and returning our
strike headquarters to us. These developments indicated to
us that our call for protest action would in itself help Local
574's cause, even though there was little chance of a general
walkout actually taking place.

Instead of supporting the strike call, Bob Cramer used the
columns of *Labor Review* to alibi for Olson. His twisted logic
depicted the raids on the strike headquarters and "614" as
clever actions "to foil the plans of the enemies of organized
labor." At the AFL headquarters, he said, the troops "made
an inspection of the premises" after getting false reports that
arms were hidden there. Thus the National Guard had proven,
he added, that the Citizens Alliance was lying in an effort
"to arouse a situation between the guard and the strikers."

The day this nonsense appeared in *Labor Review*—August
3—the strike committee of 100 invited the AFL hacks to come
before it and explain their conduct at the time of the military
attack on the union. As the minutes note, Postal, Rainbolt,
Maloney, Grant Dunne, and I gave the committee a report
of the session with Olson at the *Labor Review* offices. Jack
Maloney expressed doubt that all the Central Labor Union
brass we found there could have assembled on a moment's
notice without any foreplanning.

In a limping way Roy Wier, the CLU organizer, tried to
explain that they had met at Cramer's office to analyze the
raids. After locating Olson, he said, they asked for an explanation of the raid on the AFL headquarters and were told
by him that it was a mistake. They only wanted to help Local 574 obtain a settlement, Wier contended, and they thought
the bosses might agree to meet with them. A skeptical strike
committee member then asked a loaded question. He wanted
to know who was on the CLU committee that had asked for
the troops to be called out after the bosses rejected the Haas-
Dunnigan proposal. Cramer, who tried to answer the question, had been caught off guard, and he became quite flustered.
He wound up denying he knew who composed the committee
in question. Indirectly and by inadvertence he was actually
admitting that there had been CLU collusion with Olson behind the back of Local 574.

A motion was then adopted by the strike committee asking
that a delegation from the Central Labor Union meet with
the governor to demand removal of the troops from the city

and the release of strikers held in the military stockade. It was stipulated that the delegation would have no power to negotiate for Local 574. After that, Cramer, Wier, and the others from the CLU were excused from the meeting with the assurance that they were welcome to come again. The strike committee's attitude toward the AFL business agents was akin to the verdict once rendered by a frontier jury: "We find the defendants not guilty and we warn them not to do it again."

Front page of the August 1, 1934, Minneapolis Tribune reporting the occupation of Local 574's headquarters. Photo shows V. R. Dunne being taken into custody by National Guardsmen.

Left to right: Bill Brown, Farrell Dobbs, and Carl Skoglund.

Left to right: the Dunne Brothers: V. R., Grant, and Miles.

Above: Marvel Scholl, organizer of local 574's Women's Auxiliary. Left: Bill Brown, Miles Dunne, and V. R. Dunne leaving stockade.

Above: Governor Floyd B. Olson with federal mediators Rev. Francis J. Haas and E. H. Dunnigan. Below: National Guardsmen deployed by Olson in order to "make the city of Minneapolis as quiet as a Sunday school."

War of Attrition

At the very time Governor Olson's troops were invading the strike headquarters on the morning of August 1, 1934, John Belor died of wounds received on Bloody Friday. He was an unemployed worker who supported the strike as a member of the Minneapolis Central Council of Workers. Since John was unmarried, his nearest relatives took over burial arrangements. They asked that there be no demonstration, adding that all union members were invited to the funeral, which they wished to have conducted as quietly as possible. Honoring the relatives' request, Local 574 simply paid the burial expenses and helped to arrange transportation. Thousands of strikers joined the funeral procession to show their respect for John Belor as a fighter and to demonstrate their appreciation of the help they were getting from unemployed workers like him.

These workers had been struck a direct blow by Olson's declaration of martial law. Federal officials used it as a weapon against the strike on "made-work" projects run by the Emergency Relief Administration. An ERA directive was issued asserting that the projects would resume operations under military protection and that the provost marshal of the state guard would "apprehend agitators." Under these conditions it became necessary to call off the ERA strike on July 30. In doing so, the strike committee urged all the workers involved to join the Minneapolis Central Council of Workers and its membership soon climbed to above 4,000. The MCCW forces, of whom John Belor was an example, stood shoulder to shoulder with Local 574 on the day of the military raids, as they had done on Bloody Friday.

There were practical reasons for the affinity between Local 574 and the unemployed movement. Within the trucking industry some employees had to rely in part on public assistance. Many jobs were seasonal, and there were cases in which the earnings of regularly employed workers were too low to support a family. As a result, workers caught in such situations felt a close kinship with the totally unemployed. The feeling was reciprocated by the jobless who saw in the fighting policies of Local 574 a chance to do something about their own plight. This was before the developing labor struggles of the 1930s had compelled the boss class to make grudging concessions in the form of unemployment insurance and other social-security measures of a limited nature. In 1934 the needy were wholly dependent on public relief.

The relief system operated like something out of colonial days. Applicants were required to strip themselves down to an absolute poverty level. Any money they might have saved had to be used up and their insurance policies cashed in for the surrender value. Home appliances and other "luxury" items had to be gotten rid of via pawn shops and secondhand furniture stores. Money thus raised had to be reported and the relief budget was reduced by that amount. The budget itself was a pittance, allowing only for the bare rudiments of living. Some improvements in the relief system had been won after Local 574 began its fight against the status quo, but there was still a long way to go on that battlefront. No one understood that better than the unemployed workers and they were prepared to stand in firm solidarity with the union, come hell or high water.

The development of a new stage in the unemployed struggle came as a blow to the local Stalinists. Earlier they had acquired some influence among the jobless by setting up an organization known as Unemployed Councils. What little hold they had thus gained was now slipping fast. Contributing to their own discreditment, they falsely represented their councils as the place of registration for unemployed who wanted picket credentials in Local 574's strike. The union repudiated their assertion, stating publicly that such pickets should register with the MCCW.

When the ERA strike began after Bloody Friday, Sam Davis of the Communist Party tried to muscle his way onto the strike committee. He had no credentials from any work project, and the ERA strikers refused to seat him on their committee. Having isolated themselves from the class struggle raging in Minneapolis because of their ultraleft policies, the Stalinists reacted by continuing to denounce the "anti-working class policy of the Trotzkyite leaders." Diatribes by William F. Dunne in the *Daily Worker* were matched by the fulminations of Morris Childs in the *Communist,* a Stalinist magazine. Later their articles were put together in a pamphlet under the title, "Permanent Counter-Revolution— The role of the Trotzkyites in the Minneapolis Strike."

Giving the carping Stalinists the back of the union's hand in its issue of August 7, *The Organizer* said in an editorial: "The epic battle of Local 574 is a drama to stir the souls of men. It conforms to the classic pattern, even to the extent of having a clown and a touch of comedy. The name of this clown is, according to the leaflet surreptitiously distributed at our great mass meeting last night, 'The Communist Party of the USA, District No. 9'. . . . The leaders of our union, they say, are double-dyed traitors and the way to win the strike is to get rid of them. Some of the boys, who have been reading the same thing in the statements of the Citizens Alliance, got sore and tore up the leaflets and gave the distributors a crack on the jaw. That's wrong. Such serious treatment should be reserved for serious opponents. They are not stool pigeons— at least, not conscious ones; they are just a little bit nutty and what they need is a friendly boot in the posterior. Maybe the shock will bring them to their senses."

Meanwhile, in the real world of the time, Governor Olson was trying to recover from political damage he had suffered because of the military assault on Local 574. On August 3 he sent a small detail of guardsmen to raid the offices of the Citizens Alliance. It was a patently demagogic act, calculated to picture him as the "impartial" governor of "all the people." Local 574 shrugged the episode off for what it was, but the bosses yelled like their throats were cut. "Their" guard had been used for an "unauthorized" purpose.

By its very nature the National Guard is a strikebreaking instrument, intended for use by the bosses against the workers. To assure reliability its key officers are generally men of wealth and social position, blood brothers to the whole capitalist class. Such was the case in Minnesota, then as now, except that a few junior officers were Farmer-Laborites. One of them, Lieutenant Kenneth Haycraft, was put in charge of the raid. But that was apparently offset by other officers giving the Citizens

Alliance an advance tip-off so incriminating evidence could be spirited away. In any case, nothing of any significance came to light as a result of Olson's caper, even though the *Labor Review* painted it up as a great prolabor deed.

Parallel with this episode a real problem was developing for the Citizens Alliance. Some of the fruit and produce houses in the market district were threatening to break discipline and sign the Haas-Dunnigan proposal, which the union had accepted. This prompted the Employers' Advisory Committee to try to offset this capitulatory mood through a new proposal for settlement of the strike. The only thing really new in it was a concrete wage offer of fifty cents an hour for truck drivers and forty cents an hour for helpers and inside workers. The representation clause in the new proposal continued to omit any mention of Local 574. A "preferential" hiring list was still insisted upon, putting scabs ahead of union members, and strikers accused of "unlawful" acts were not to be rehired.

Local 574 immediately rejected the employers' proposal, stating that it would accept nothing less than the original Haas-Dunnigan terms. The union had won victories on the picket line, *The Organizer* declared, and it was not going to be cheated out of them in negotiations. Attention was called to the fact that a critical period had been reached in the strike. The workers were up against enemies who were full of tricks. There was only one course for Local 574 to follow, the union paper said. That was continuation and extension of its picketing activities.

At about this juncture one picketing incident got out of hand. Bill Brown and Grant Dunne, who were walking along a street near the strike headquarters, spotted a scab truck with a military permit. Commandeering a couple of cruising picket squads, they set out to stop it, and the driver produced a shotgun. In the ensuing melee they let their impulsiveness get the better of sound tactical judgment. As a result two pickets were wounded, Earl Collins and George Schirtz. When Kelly Postal heard what had happened he was fit to be tied. He had good reason because, as picket dispatcher, he was in command of tactical operations. Bill and Grant had superseded his authority, vetoed general orders to avoid incidents of that kind, and got two strikers shot for no useful purpose.

Although the episode could not be allowed to disrupt the strike, action had to be taken in order to demonstrate that union discipline applied to the leadership as well as the ranks.

The strike committee did so by instructing Bill and Grant—
who were among the top union leaders—to subordinate themselves to Kelly in matters concerning his function as chief
picket dispatcher. Knowing they were in the wrong, Bill and
Grant took the rebuke as gracefully as they could, and there
was no repetition of such conduct.

Uncontrolled fighting of that kind, aimed at random scab
operations, would not serve as a helpful tactic. It would only
put the union in a bad propaganda light. Our proper course
was to keep the political heat on Olson, demanding that he
stop giving military permits to scab trucks, and cease interfering with Local 574's right to picket peacefully. This had
been done in issue after issue of *The Organizer,* and it was
generating mass pressure on the governor. He felt compelled
to announce that, as of August 6, he would revoke all military permits; new ones would be issued only to signers of
the Haas-Dunnigan terms and to "emergency" cases.

The Citizens Alliance reacted by seeking a federal court injunction against the continuance of martial law. On numerous
occasions before this the bosses had gotten court orders against
Local 574, and the union had ignored them on the premise
that the cops couldn't make the orders stick. It was different
in Olson's case, the Citizens Alliance obviously felt, expecting
him to obey an injunction if one could be obtained. Hoping
to regain direct control of the strikebreaking efforts, the bosses
imported thugs from the P. L. Bergoff agency, a notorious
scab-herding outfit based in New York.

Local 574 took the position that the legal squabble between
the governor and the employers was a private affair of their
own. We never asked for martial law, the union said, and
we don't want it now. Demands were repeated that union members be freed from the stockade and that the military stop
interfering with peaceful picketing. *Local 574's fundamental
line was declared to remain one of independent and militant
struggle by the workers.*

The strike committee was prepared for whatever decision
the court made in the injunction case. As *The Organizer* noted:
"If the martial regime is sustained, they [the strikers] will continue to fight along the lines of the past week. . . . If martial law is supended, pickets will immediately take the field
in force and tie up all trucking as Local 574 has repeatedly
shown it can do without difficulty and without violence." As
it turned out, the court sustained the martial regime.

On the evening of August 6, Local 574 held an open rally at the Parade Grounds with 40,000 workers present, a record-breaking attendance. In addressing the meeting the union leaders had several objectives in mind. It was necessary to dispel illusions that Citizens Alliance opposition to martial law showed there was something good about it for the workers. Mass pressure had to be kept on Olson to slow down his piecemeal strikebreaking through military permits. An alert was needed against the importation by the bosses of hired thugs and professional scabs. An answer had to be given to the intensified red-baiting attack on the Local 574 leadership.

The workers had rejected the smear campaign against the leaders not through any basic political understanding of the need for a nonexclusion policy in mass organizations. Their attitude flowed from the realities of the given situation. The union members were consulted about everything that was done, and they believed in the policies that were being followed. They didn't care what the leaders were politically. What counted for them was that the guidance they were getting had stood the test of battle time and again. The workers had confidence in the leaders, and they wanted no change.

After the rally *The Organizer* of August 8 took up the red-baiting issue in a rather unique way. Under the title, "A Bughouse Fable," it published a simulated confession by the editor, who had supposedly been dragged into Olson's military court. Written by Jim Cannon, the "confession" said in part:

"OFFICER: Who's dis guy called Father Haas? . . .

"EDITOR: His real name is Haasky. He's a Russian bolshevik. . . . His proposal of 42 1/2 cents an hour is practically the same thing as Communism. . . .

"OFFICER: Spill the rest of it. What about Dunnigan, Olson, Brown and the Dunne brothers — how many of these here Dunne brothers is there all told?

"EDITOR: Their real name is Dunnskovitsky. They are Irish Jews from County Cork, smuggled into the country about six months ago disguised as sacks of Irish potatoes. There are seventeen of them in Minneapolis, all the same age, and they all holler for 42 1/2 cents an hour. They say that's the beginning of Communism. . . . Mr. Dunnigan's right name is Dunnigansky — a cousin of the Dunne boys and hand in glove with them on the 42 1/2 cents an hour racket.

"OFFICER: What about Brown?

"EDITOR: He's a Jew named Bronstein, a fish peddler from

the east side of New York. He came here a few weeks ago
and tried to sell Bismark herring down at the market. Then
he lined up with the Dunnskovitskys and muscled into the
union racket, and got himself elected president of Local 574.
. . . By the way, he is a son of Leon Bronstein—that's the
original name of this guy Trotsky that started all the trouble
over in Russia.

"OFFICER: How about Governor Olson? He's in wit youse
guys in the Communist racket, ain't he?

"EDITOR: Sure! That's the slickest part of the whole game.
That guy's a card. His right name is not Olson, and he's
not a Swede either—that's just a gag to get the Scandinavian
vote. He's a Russian importation—direct from Moscow—and
his real name is Olsonovich. He's been a big help to the strike.
That raid he pulled off at the union headquarters and the
throwing of the pickets in the stockade, was all a trick to get
sympathy for the strikers.

"OFFICER: This is gettin' too deep for me. Who cooked
up this whole scheme, anyway?

"EDITOR: Well, to tell the truth, it was all planned out in
Constantinople a few months ago. Some of the boys worked
a week driving trucks and saved up enough money to take
a trip to Europe. They went to Constantinople to see Trotsky
and get instructions for their next move. Trotsky said: 'Boys,
I want a revolution in Minneapolis before the snow flies.' They
said 'O. K.' and started to leave.

"Just as they were about to take the boat, Vincent Dunne
stepped up to old man Trotsky and said: 'What's your last
word of advice before we go?'

"OFFICER: What did Trotsky say?

"EDITOR: He said: 'Boys, keep your eye on Olsonovich.
He is liable to double cross you any minute.'"

This lampoon of the red-baiters, with its pointed barbs at
the governor, was received with belly laughs throughout the
labor movement. The reception helped to set the stage for
yet another blow at the bosses through *The Organizer.* Under
a headline, "Here Are the 166 Tyrants," the paper published
a complete list of the trucking firms who were fighting the
union. The information was provided, it said, "for those who
like to know where they spend their money." Requests quickly
came from throughout the region that the list be republished
for the benefit of those who hadn't seen it the first time. A
boycott movement of the most effective kind rapidly developed,

one tied directly to a hard-fought strike struggle. While the fight couldn't be won that way, the boycott could at least complicate things for the Citizens Alliance. It did, in fact, help to push three market firms among the 166 into breaking Citizens Alliance discipline and signing the original Haas-Dunnigan terms.

With this crack appearing in their ranks, the bosses issued a public blast against Haas and Dunnigan. They demanded that Washington recall the mediators, on the ground that they were "playing into the hands of the radical leadership of the truck drivers' union." Haas and Dunnigan buckled under the attack, abandoned their original settlement terms, and tried to help the bosses impose harsher conditions on the strikers. Their changed position focused on two points: (a) abandonment of any specific minimum wage; and (b) a provision that the bosses could challenge the rehiring of strikers accused of "violence."

The mediators began their new push by trying to put pressure on Ray Dunne and me, the union negotiating committee. Washington insisted on a settlement, they said, and the union would have to give some ground. They demanded that we recommend their new terms to the membership, saying they would go to the ranks themselves if we refused. Ray and I merely said that we would report to the union what had transpired in our talk with them.

A decision was made to grant the mediators' request that they be allowed to appear before the strike committee. When they arrived, they were kept waiting outside the meeting room until the committee was ready to receive them. Ray and I first gave the body a report of the mediators' new pitch, recounting what had been said in our talk with them. It was also reported that strike-committee members in the stockade had already been informed of the new development, after which they had voted to reject the changed settlement terms. The proposition was then put to the committee as a whole, and it was turned down unanimously.

At this point, Haas and Dunnigan were granted permission to enter the meeting. None of the top leaders took the floor until other members of the committee had worked them over. Typical of the many questions put to the mediators were these: "Why do you go over the heads of our negotiating committee and not over the heads of the bosses' negotiating committee? Why don't you force the 166 to take a secret ballot on your

original settlement plan? Will the man from Washington who
judges 'violence' cases wear a white collar or overalls?"

After this round had been completed the top leaders spoke.
Ray Dunne did the main job of tearing apart the mediators'
new proposal and reaffirming the union's position about settlement terms. During the discussion Bill Brown delivered a
stinging rebuke to Haas and Dunnigan. "We have been fighting
for four weeks," he said. "All of us have sacrificed and strug-
gled; two of our brothers lie dead at the hands of the bosses'
agents. We accepted your first plan. And now you ask us to
bow our heads and go back to the old slavery, and you would
speak of fairness and honor?" In reporting Bill's remarks
The Organizer noted that he had moved the committee to wild
applause. Finally the mediators asked to be excused from the
meeting. As Father Haas was leaving the room, a young
Catholic worker ripped away a crucifix suspended around
his neck and hurled it at the departing priest.

Having failed to get their way through pressure on the federal mediators, the bosses devised a new scheme. They started
a petition campaign for a Labor Board election, allegedly
to determine whether or not the workers wanted Local 574
to negotiate a settlement of the strike. Voting was to be confined to employees certified as "eligible" by the bosses. Beneath
the tricky legal wording of the petition lay the slick aim of
rigging the outcome by padding the election lists with scab
voters. The Labor Board was to be used as a front to get
the federal government's endorsement of the strikebreaking
move. Local 574 immediately organized a counter-campaign
to expose the fraud, but the bosses kept chipping away, trying
to make a breakthrough with their petitions.

While this was going on Governor Olson again loosened up
the permit system. Before long thousands of trucks were being
allowed on the streets with military approval, no more than
a third of them owned by signers of the Haas-Dunnigan terms.
Union interference with the scab operations brought military
arrest of pickets. They were sentenced to hard labor at the
stockade, some for as much as ninety days. When Marvel
Scholl was sent to cover the military trials as a reporter for
The Organizer, the presiding officer had her ejected from the
court room.

Conditions in the makeshift stockade were deplorable. They
were described in an *Organizer* editorial entitled, "The Stockade
is a Hog-lot!" The prisoners were herded into overcrowded

tents with insufficient blankets. Tasteless food, brought in an open truck, arrived cold. Toilet facilities were primitive and fly-infested. Bathing facilities consisted of rusty dishpans and a hose. And copies of the union paper were confiscated by the stockade guards. Being the fighters they were, the imprisoned pickets organized themselves and gradually won better conditions.

At this juncture in the developing war of attrition, Local 574 called for a general demonstration strike. "Bring up the labor reserves," *The Organizer* urged in an appeal to the rest of the trade-union movement. The Minneapolis Central Labor Union was asked to add its voice in a request for support from the Minnesota State Federation of Labor which was to hold a convention on August 20. As had happened after the military raid on the strike headquarters, the appeal fell on deaf ears among conservative AFL officials. They knew that the demonstration would be against Olson as well as the bosses, since his troops were doing the main strikebreaking job. Being incapable of putting the interests of the strikers above everything else, the AFL business agents were determined at all hazards to defend the governor against his critics within the labor movement. They were also beginning to lend off-the-record encouragement to cautious internal challenges of the Local 574 leadership.

On August 9 Cliff Hall went on the prod at a strike-committee meeting. He was still nominally the business agent for Local 574 and he announced some decisions made by the official executive board. Asserting that the board had full power over the strike committee, he said it had decided to vacate the strike headquarters on August 16 because there wasn't enough money to continue paying the rent. He also said that, as an "official" union answer to the red-baiting, a majority of the board members had issued a press statement. It turned out to be a weasel-worded apology calculated to appease the witch-hunters by pleading that no member of the union was a member of the Communist Party.

A motion was adopted by the strike committee instructing the organizing committee (Ray, Miles, and Grant Dunne, Carl Skoglund, and myself) to meet with the executive board and settle this matter. The joint meeting of the organizing committee and the executive board was immediately held. As the minutes show, a motion was adopted that, "the orders of the strike committee are not to be countermanded by the executive board, inasmuch as the executive board sits in the strike committee and may voice objections there." A second motion was also passed that "the [organizing] committee of five also be included in the executive board meetings."

When these decisions were reported to the next strike-committee session, another hassle developed. Sam Haskell, the secretary-treasurer, contended that he was the only one with power to make expenditures. Hall then repeated his assertion that the executive board had supreme authority over the union. Carl Skoglund blasted them, pointing out that the union membership was the supreme authority. The members, he emphasized, had authorized the strike committee to act for them and it was therefore empowered to give orders to the executive board. After the debate had ended, the strike committee adopted a motion that "the strike committee, sitting together with the executive board, rule on all policies of the union, including all expenditures of monies, and that all strike committee decisions be final for the duration of the strike." Although defeated in the strike committee, Hall and his cronies didn't give up. They simply went underground, peddling their red-baiting gossip to whoever would listen in the union ranks and among members of the womens auxiliary.

A similarly underhanded attack also came from another quarter. John Geary, a general organizer of Tobin's, began to connive with a handful of independent taxi owners. Their aim was to reestablish the small local union of cab drivers, which had been liquidated into Local 574 when the Yellow Cab drivers were organized during the May strike. Their immediate object was to get their cabs back on the streets. When Local 574 got wind of the move a meeting was called of the independent taxi owners and their relief drivers. After the situation was thrashed out and the splitting move understood for what it was, a majority of those at the meeting voted to stay in Local 574 and remain on strike.

Not long thereafter a blow came from the national AFL headquarters, one that had the earmarks of being arranged by Tobin. Filling-station attendants were being organized into Local 574, along with the truck drivers for the oil companies. Since the companies were negotiating with the union these workers had not been called out on strike. It would seem reasonable that any jurisdictional questions in such a situation be held in abeyance while Local 574 was fighting for its life, but that wasn't the case.

Paul Smith, an agent of William Green, the AFL president, was sent from Washington to put the filling-station attendants into a separate union right then and there. He proceeded with the attempt behind the back of Local 574, in the middle of its strike against the trucking bosses. Smith called a meeting for that purpose, bringing a dozen detectives to the hall with him for protection.

Although Local 574 received no invitation it sent a delegation to the meeting led by Grant Dunne. When Smith saw them he became hesitant to start the meeting so Grant took over the chair. The detectives were ordered removed from the meeting and Smith scurried out with them. Grant and the other representatives from our strike committee then left, turning the meeting over to the filling-station operators themselves. They decided to stay with Local 574, at least for the duration of the strike, but later on we had to agree to their reorganization into a separate AFL union.

As the strike wore on, money problems became increasingly severe. Although the Farmers' Holiday Association came through handsomely on its promise to keep the commissary supplied with meat and vegetables, we still had to spend about $500 a day for other food items. Gasoline for the cruising squads came to another $400 daily and with medicines and incidentals included, it cost around $1,000 a day to keep the strike going. The problem was eased some by large donations from other unions. Milk Drivers Local 471 gave us $6,000. Typographical Union Local 42 came through with $1,000 for the commissary, and it pledged $250 a week for the duration of the walkout to help publish *The Organizer*. Another $1,000 was received from the Cooks and Waiters Union, which was holding its national convention in Minneapolis. A steady trickle of small contributions came from individual workers, and funds were also raised by touring the state with the picket truck that had been shot up on Bloody Friday.

Like the union, individual strikers were finding the going rougher and rougher. Children were being poorly fed. Lights, gas, and water were in numerous instances shut off for nonpayment of bills. Rent problems became increasingly acute. Fighting the city administration to get relief for strikers had developed into one of our biggest tasks. On top of all that the real-estate interests launched a drive to evict strikers from their homes for delinquencies in rent. In many cases we man-

aged to turn the latter around by scraping up a month's rent
on a new house and using picket trucks to move the ousted
families. This action bought at least another month of time,
if not a bit more, and eliminated any need to pay back rent.

All in all, the union was in a pretty worn state. We had
been in almost constant battle since May. More and more
trucks were moving under military permits. A few of the
strikers were beginning to give up hope and trickle back to
work. A new federal mediator, P. A. Donoghue, was being
sent from Washington to replace Haas and Dunnigan. He
was getting a press buildup as a hotshot, and he might well
be coming to help the bosses put through the phoney election they wanted. It was becoming a very difficult situation.

Al Goldman pointed this out at a special meeting he had
asked for with Jim Cannon, Carl Skoglund, Ray Dunne, and
me—the five of us constituting the party steering committee
in the strike. Al argued that we were beaten and had to throw
in the towel. In one sense he had raised a legitimate point.
When a strike is being defeated there is no percentage in keeping every militant on the picket line to the very last. In such a
case it is better to have some of the fighters go back to work,
as though they were quitting the strike, with the hope they can
be in a position to prepare for another battle later on.

If Al had simply posed the question on that basis for consideration, it would have been in order for him to do so. Instead he began to argue strongly that the strike must be called
off at once. I felt that he went too far in pressing for such
a decision. Although he had been on the scene for a little over
a month, he did not have as good a feel of the mood in the
ranks as did Ray, Carl, and I—those of us who had been
in intimate touch with the union membership for much longer
and through many fights. I felt that a person coming into
the situation from the outside, as was the case with Al, should
not have been so categorical about such a life-and-death question for the union. I wasn't the only one who felt that way.
Carl Skoglund took the lead in arguing for continuance of
the strike. Ray Dunne joined in with him, as did I, and we had
a hot debate. Jim Cannon, who had more practical strike
experience than Al Goldman, first listened very carefully to
our arguments. Then he said he considered it a key fact that
the leaders in closest touch with the ranks still thought the
strike could be won.

It was not alone a question of the union being worn down

we felt. The bosses were not as fresh as daisies either. We knew they were putting pressure on the Citizens Alliance to let them make a settlement with the workers. If we could hang on for a longer time, there was still a good chance that the union could win.

By the time the argument was over, Goldman had changed his mind, seeming to gain renewed confidence from our insistence that the strike should continue. A slogan was formulated for publication in the Organizer: "Local 574 will not stand for fake elections." The union demands that no elections be held, we stated in an editorial, unless all strikers are first returned to work without discrimination. A union victory in the elections, we insisted, would have to mean that the bosses were required to recognize Local 574 and meet all the conditions of the Haas-Dunnigan plan.

Local 574 Wins

Our more optimistic estimate of the situation was confirmed by the way in which the long battle suddenly came to an end. The new federal mediator, P. A. Donoghue, had not come from Washington to rig a fake election as we had suspected might be his aim. Instead it seemed that President Roosevelt has decided to help Governor Olson get the strike off his hands before the November elections. This was in order since the Farmer-Labor Party administration was supporting the Roosevelt Democrats in national politics.

As a new mediator, Donoghue was in a position to communicate Roosevelt's wishes to the bosses and at the same time give them a face-saving device by superseding Haas and Dunnigan in the negotiations. Whatever his instructions were, Donoghue got right down to business. On August 21, 1934, he submitted a new proposal to the union for settlement of the strike. In doing so, he told us "off the record" that he had convinced A. W. Strong, head of the Citizens Alliance, to call off the fight. We demanded something more explicit about the bosses' attitude before submitting the new proposal to the union membership. Donoghue responded then and there by dictating and signing a letter that stated: "This is to advise you that the Employers have consented to having the Minneapolis-St. Paul Regional Labor Board enter a consent order containing the proposal submitted to you this afternoon." Since a settlement now appeared in the offing, the union also demanded that Governor Olson put in writing a promise to release all pickets from the stockade, which he did.

Under the terms of the consent order to which Donoghue referred, the Labor Board was to conduct a collective-bargaining election within ten days. Only employees on the payroll as of July 16, the day before the strike began, were to vote; no voting by scabs was to be allowed. In firms where

Local 574 won a majority in the balloting, it was to be recognized as the bargaining agent for all employees, and the employers were to be required to deal with it.

On the inside-worker issue, which had led to the July-August strike, the breakthrough made in the original Haas-Dunnigan plan was reaffirmed. The twenty-two market firms were to recognize the union's right to represent drivers, helpers, platform workers, and inside workers. Inside workers were defined as all employees within the establishment, except office workers and salesmen. As had been stated in the earlier proposal, union representation was to be more restricted in the remainder of the 166 firms for whom the Employers' Advisory Committee spoke. Employees included in these cases were limited to drivers, helpers, and platform workers directly engaged in loading and unloading trucks. On this point we still had the opinion that a victorious union could establish de facto representation of all its members, even though a few were not explicitly included in the terms of the settlement.

For the first time since the union demands were originally presented, the bosses were definitely committing themselves to specific figures on minimum-wage rates. No less than fifty cents an hour was to be paid to truck drivers and forty cents an hour to helpers, platform workers, and inside workers. It was stipulated that any current wage rates above these minimums were not to be reduced. Provision was made for arbitration of the union's demand for higher minimum-pay scales.

The board of arbitration was to consist of two union representatives, two employer representatives, and a fifth party to be chosen by these four. After the Labor Board election had determined the union representation issue, the board of arbitration judgements were to be applied retroactively to the time of arbitration. All employees were to be reinstated in their jobs, without discrimination, on the basis of seniority. There was to be neither "preferential" employment of scabs, nor "violence" gimmicks to victimize strikers.

Although the settlement provided much less than the workers deserved, it was as much as we could get at the time. On the whole the gains that were being registered provided a solid basis from which to go forward with the union-building job. From these considerations it followed that the leadership should recommend approval of the settlement by the union members. A session of the strike committee of 100 was immediately called to consider the new turn of events. It voted to ask acceptance of the proposed terms which were to be submitted to a membership meeting that same evening, August 21. I was assigned to report the proposal to the body when it assembled and to recommend its adoption.

Rumors of the impending end of the strike had been flying, and the gathering virtually breathed a sense of relief that the battle was about over. As is usual in the mass movement, there were also a few present who wanted to fight on to the bitter end for more substantial concessions from the bosses. Among them was a worker who showed signs of having stopped by a beer joint on his way to the meeting. I had no more finished my report when he asked for the floor. "That doesn't meet the demands we went on strike for," he said. "What's the matter with Brother Dobbs, has he lost his guts?"

His attitude was an exception to the general feeling among the strikers, as was evidenced in the discussion that followed. All that the leaders really had to do was to put the outcome of the strike into perspective concerning the future it promised for the union. The settlement terms were accepted almost unanimously and the jubilant meeting adjourned with the singing of "Solidarity Forever."

After almost five weeks of bitter conflict, coming on the heels of the hard-fought May strike, the workers had won a sweeping victory. Growing realization of what had been accomplished was reflected in the mood back at strike headquarters after the membership meeting was over. A good example was the pride with which Brother Sloan did his announcing over the loudspeaker. Sloan, whom we called "Brother" as a nickname, said in signing off: "This is Station 574 broadcasting, with 7,500 pickets, 450 cruiser cars, 16 motorcycles and 2 airplanes, by authority of the Strike Committee of 100."

In an editorial hailing the union victory, *The Organizer* took note that "the strike ends but the struggle does not end." It warned that the bosses would be up to their usual sneaky tricks in the Labor Board elections to be held on August 28. There were to be two opposing tickets: Local 574's and a company-union slate. Several employer devices were used in an effort to steal the elections. Payroll lists were padded with office workers and salesmen. Attempts were made to leave some union members off the list. There were also cases in which a boss tried to put the name of a good union member on the company-union slate.

To combat these maneuvers Local 574 organized for the elections as it had prepared for the strike, using *The Organizer* as the main weapon. Daily publication of the union paper continued throughout the preelection period. (After the elections, *The Organizer* continued briefly as a weekly and publication was then suspended for lack of funds.) As reports came in from union members of each boss trick, the paper would publish a general alert and explain how to combat the underhanded move. The union campaign was climaxed by a big open rally the night before the vote. Nonmembers from within the industry were invited and the speakers explained in a friendly way why these workers should vote for the victorious union and join it.

The election returns made Local 574 the bargaining representative for 61 percent of the employees in the general trucking industry. Majority votes gave the union the right to speak for all employees in sixty-two firms. At fifteen companies there were tie votes. In these cases Local 574 had the right to represent its half of the employees, thereby gaining union recognition on these jobs. At nearly all the large companies the workers voted about three to one for Local 574, and the bloc of twenty-two market firms went solidly for the union. The boss slates won a majority at sixty-eight places. These were generally small outfits, which usually operated on a paternalistic, sort of semi-family basis. At twenty-one companies no votes were cast at all. These firms had not been organized by Local 574, but they had nevertheless joined in with the rest of the 166 in the war against the union. All in all, the union had established itself in virtually every branch of the trucking industry.

Right after the elections, the union filed a request for arbitration, seeking to raise the minimum-wage rates above those provided in the strike settlement. Grant Dunne and I were assigned to represent the union on the board of arbitration. Various employer representatives were selected, company by company. John R. Coan, a local lawyer, was agreed upon as the "impartial" fifth member of the board. A wage decision was to be made concerning each of the seventy-seven establishments where the union had either won a majority or got a tie vote. The sections of the industry involved were: transfer, market, lumber, coffee, furniture, wholesale grocery, hardware and plumbing, spring water, lime and cement, packing, paint and glass, paper, and retailers.

As a pilot case, the Employers' Advisory Committee selected
a transfer company. After the union and the bosses had argued
the case in the board, Coan made an award in favor of Local
574. Truck drivers were granted a minimum of 52 1/2¢ an
hour from September 15, 1934 to May 31, 1935, and 55¢
an hour from June 1, 1935, to May 31, 1936. Minimum scales
of 42 1/2¢ and 45¢ for the same two periods were specified
for helpers, platform workers, and inside workers.

What Coan had done was to apply the Haas-Dunnigan proposal to the first stage and bring wage rates up to the union's
prestrike demand in the second. His decision reflected the pressures generated by Local 574's terrific battle. Inclusion of inside workers in the ruling—when the strike settlement called
only for our representation of drivers, helpers, and platform
workers at a transfer company—confirmed our estimate of
the impact of the union victory. It meant formal recognition
of our right to represent warehousemen, furniture packers,
etc., and set a precedent for comparable expansion of our
right to represent all union members at other companies.
After the arbitration decision in the transfer case, the union
established the same wage rates in direct talks with the market firms. Following that the Employers' Advisory Committee announced that all the seventy-seven companies were accepting the Coan ruling on wages.

Our agreement to carry out this arbitration procedure was
strictly a tactical decision arising from the complexities of the
conflict. The key issues were union recognition and the right
to represent all union members. We would not have agreed
to arbitrate either of these basic points. As a matter of fact
we had denounced Governor Olson's proposal, after the May
strike, that the inside-worker issue be arbitrated. These were
matters that had to be fought to a finish. The limited concession we had made on the inside-worker question in accepting
the original Haas-Dunnigan proposal resulted from the bad
bind in which the union was caught at the time. We still intended to fight in some other way to regain the ground that
circumstances had forced us to yield, and we were confident
a victory in the strike would make that possible.

Seemingly aware of our determination in this matter, and
not being eager for another fight soon with the union, the
bosses yielded on this point in accepting the Coan ruling.
Although the union welcomed as a windfall Coan's expansion
of the inside-worker definition, we would have rejected any

attempt on his part to freeze the scope of union representation
through his ruling. For us that was not an arbitratable matter.
Since union recognition was the paramount issue in the fierce
battle with the bosses, we could afford to be somewhat flexible
on the wage issue insofar as that might help to win on the
main point. Any setback on the wage question arising from
this tactical course would be only limited and temporary. Once
the union was firmly established on the job, the workers would
have a solid foundation for a steady advance in wages and
working conditions. These considerations led us to accept wage
arbitration, so that the main thrust of the strike could be focused on the issue of union recognition. Our decision in no
way implied agreement with the outlook and practices of the
average union business agent. Unlike such misleaders, we
were not trying to substitute arbitration for strike action in an
effort to get the bosses to accept us as "labor statesmen."

We fully understood that there is no such animal as an "impartial" arbitrator in worker-capitalist disputes. There is actually no middle ground in such situations and no one stands
unaffected by the conflicts that occur. Arbitrators—who are
usually lawyers, jurists, preachers, etc.—have left a long trail
across the years of being "neutral" on the capitalist side. Their
sorry record stems from their acceptance of ruling-class norms
coupled with a desire to get ahead themselves in the capitalist
world. These considerations make them susceptible to many
forms of pressure from the boss class. At best, arbitrators
will make only timid concessions to the unions and then only
under heavy counterpressure from the working class.

For these reasons workers should avoid arbitration of their
demands wherever possible. In dealing with basic issues, it
should be resorted to only under highly unusual circumstances:
for example, in an effort to salvage some employer concessions
out of an otherwise lost strike. Where secondary points are submitted to arbitration for tactical considerations, it should be
looked upon as a necessary evil rather than a desirable procedure. Agreement to arbitrate grievances arising from employer violations of a union contract is a highly dangerous
course for the workers. What usually happens is that the grievances pile up behind the arbitration dam, and the boss gets
away with murder. On this point, Local 574 retained the un-
conditional right to strike in accepting the August 21 settlement.
The union remained free to take such action to settle grievances
or for any other cause.

After the July-August strike was over, the union thanked its friends for their help. To cite some outstanding instances, Herbert Solow was made an honorary member of the union in appreciation of his work as editor of *The Organizer*. Argus press was also remembered for its courageous printing of the strike daily. Special tributes were paid to Joe Goslin, the foreman; Ace Johnston, the linotype operator; and Roy Kalstrom, the make-up man at Argus. Dr. McCrimmon became the family doctor for many union households, and after a time the union itself worked out a cooperative medical plan with him.

Joe Davis, who ran Lyons Bar near the union headquarters, also got special commendation in the form of a practical joke. He had kept collection cans on the bar to raise money for the union; we had used his phone for long-distance calls at his expense; and he had often put up bail money to spring pickets from the jug. An official telegram of thanks was sent to Joe with the following postscript: "We know you won't mind our sending this collect as funds are low." Joe later told an *Organizer* reporter, "Seeing that it brought good news, I had to tip the delivery boy two bits, so it cost me a dollar to get thanked."

E. G. Hall, president of the Minnesota State Federation of Labor, was not on our list of those to be thanked because he stabbed the union in the back the day after the strike ended. In the *Minneapolis Tribune* of August 22, 1934, he was reported to have said, "The leadership in the Minneapolis truck strike had caused turmoil by seeking to include other crafts in the drivers' union, and by promising the impossible." He was also said to have hinted broadly that a fight against "communistic tendencies" would be made inside the state AFL.

This attack by the head of the State Federation of Labor encouraged Cliff Hall to step up his red-baiting campaign inside Local 574. He was now in a somewhat better position to carry on this skulduggery. Dissolution of the strike committee after August 21 had restored formal authority to the executive board, and he still controlled a narrow majority in that body. Hall's cronies within the women's auxiliary became especially vicious in their attacks on the strike leaders. Things got so bad that something had to be done quickly. So Moe Hork introduced a motion in the executive board to disband the auxiliary, and Brown and Frosig helped to force its adoption. Moe had done good work during the strike. As this action on his part indicated, he was breaking from his earlier collaboration with Hall.

By this time it was clear that the entire Hall gang had to be cleaned out of union office before their disruption began to weaken the organization. As the first step toward that end, Bill Brown called for the resignation of all incumbent officers, including himself. The others agreed to resign, apparently thinking they could win in new elections. We put up opposition candidates for the posts held by Hall's stooges and campaigned strongly against them. When the votes were counted the following new executive board had been chosen: Bill Brown, reelected president; George Frosig, reelected vice-president; Grant Dunne, newly elected recording secretary; F. Dobbs, newly elected secretary-treasurer; Ray Dunne and Harry DeBoer, newly elected trustees; and Moe Hork, reelected trustee. Neither Miles Dunne nor Carl Skoglund had been chosen as part of our ticket. Miles had been assigned to help the Teamster's union in Fargo, North Dakota. It had not been considered wise for Carl to be a candidate because of his citizenship problem.

Incompetents holding posts on the old executive board had now been removed by the membership. They were replaced by leaders who had won rank-and-file support during the union's long struggle against the bosses. To complete the renovation, the new board promptly fired Cliff Hall as business agent. Steps were taken to develop a staff of union organizers who would conduct themselves as working-class fighters, not as "statesmenlike" AFL business agents. Having been properly timed, all this had been accomplished with the same ease that a withered husk can be stripped from a ripened ear of corn.

These changes in official leadership set the stage for further consolidation of Local 574. The former strike committee of 100 was now transformed into an instrument for union control on the job. Its members, along with former picket captains, were elected by the workers as job stewards. Their task was to enforce the strike settlement, and to crowd as far as they could beyond its specific terms in order to pave the way for advances in the next union contract. Their strike experience made them very capable stewards. With the union power standing solidly behind them, they proceeded militantly to make the bosses toe the line. At the same time they took the lead in recruiting new union members, and as part of their task, they saw to it that union dues were paid regularly.

Special attention was given to the coal workers situation. As business picked up in the fall the union fought for the return of all employees to their jobs on a seniority basis. Bosses

who had so cockily fired union militants the previous spring
now found themselves compelled to take them back — or else.
Quickie strikes in a couple of yards reformed the unbelievers.
After that it was primarily a matter of enforcing the existing
working agreement which ran to the spring of 1935.

Parallel to the concentration of attention on the coal industry,
measures were taken to develop a special section within Local
574 for unemployed workers. Leaders of the Minneapolis
Central Council of Workers hailed the step and agreed to dis-
solve their organization into the new union setup. While the
unemployed would still have their own formation as a special
section of the union, direct affiliation with Local 574 gave
them new leverage as an organic part of the official labor
movement.

The MCCW's leap in membership between May and August
had been an exceptional development, related directly to the
mass actions of the time. It was now experiencing a sharp
decline in strength due to the relative quiet following the end
of the truck drivers' walkout, but the basic cadres remained
intact. Among the latter were several figures who could do
a lot to get the new union section underway. What they needed
primarily was help from a competent political leader, but such
a person could not be spared from the union staff. If the gap
was to be filled, the Communist League would have to do it.
This key assignment was given to Max Geldman, a party
member who had transferred to the city from New York after
the July-August strike was over. He stuck to his post, did
his job well, and thereafter played a prominent role in the
Minneapolis unemployed movement.

Although the Communist League had been quick to reinforce the local comrades in a big way while the battle was
on, its limited forces precluded longer-range assignments of
personnel for the long haul in consolidating the union. For
this reason Max's arrival was more or less a windfall of which
we promptly took advantage. Since further aid of the kind
couldn't realistically be expected, we had to go forward on
our own local resources. Significant forces for the purpose were
available. By the fall of 1934 the party's Minneapolis branch
had grown to about 100 members and close sympathizers,
more than double the membership a year earlier. Recruits
had been won within various trade-union locals; also among
students and intellectuals. In the case of Local 574, a big
and growing party fraction now existed. The reasons for this

expansion can perhaps best be illustrated through a few individual examples.

Marvel Scholl, who had fought in the strikes as a member of the women's auxiliary, spoke of her political evolution in her diary: "It was on July 20, Bloody Friday, that I made up my mind, or rather my heart, to join the Communist League of America. . . . The headquarters had become a frontline battle hospital for a few hours. . . . When the last of the casualties had been taken out to the many hospitals for further treatment I slipped out, went down to the hotel where Jim Cannon and Max Shachtman had a room. Jim was alone in the room. I told him, 'I don't know what the League is all about but whatever it is, if it is against what happened today, I want to join.' Jim was gentle with me. He explained that nobody was allowed to join the party purely from emotional reasons, that they had to know what they were joining, what it stood for, what it was against, and with this knowledge, make up their minds if they wanted to devote their lives to the cause. He must have recognized my state of shock, and while he welcomed my intentions, advised that I learn what the program was, what becoming a revolutionary socialist meant. But from that day on my intentions were clear. I was put under the tutelage of Carl Skoglund. . . . It was not until after the strike was over that I was admitted to the party."

Though in a different way, Bloody Friday also had its political impact on Harry DeBoer. As he later described his situation, "I wound up with forty-five pounds of weights hanging on my leg and guards to see that I didn't run away!" Once the surgery was over and his long convalescence began, Harry had a lot of unoccupied time on his hands. Fellow strikers came to see him when they could, among them party members with whom he was able to have political discussions.

Oscar Coover, Sr., brought him volume one of Marx's basic work *Capital* to read. It's a hefty volume to handle when lying on one's back, and besides Harry wasn't much of a reading man at the time. He preferred to talk politics with those whose views he respected and he did a lot of thinking. Out of it all came a decision on his part to join the Communist League. In explaining his action he made a broad political generalization about Local 574's victory that is hard to improve upon: "We couldn't have done it without a disciplined revolutionary party."

Bill Brown also came to consider himself a Trotskyist. Even though this did not lead him to active membership in the Communist League, no political hesitation on his part was necessarily implied. I, personally, thought that his attitude showed the depth of his respect for the party. Bill was an undisciplined person, and he seemed to know himself well enough to realize that this wouldn't change simply because he joined the League. If we tried to convince him otherwise, he might well have wound up making a problem of himself as a formal member. As it was, he played an invaluable role as a close sympathizer. He collaborated loyally and consistently with the party fraction on all important matters within Local 574. Whenever a national party figure came through the city on a speaking tour, Bill would be on hand to hear the talk, and part of what he heard would often find its way into the next major speech of his own within the union movement. He was also generous about making financial contributions to the party, insisting that we take for granted his adherence to this particular obligation of party membership.

With Local 574 in bad financial shape after the strike, union staff got at most twenty dollars a week each, sometimes less. Out of this sum, party members on the staff had decided that we would each contribute a dollar a week to the party branch. An incident in this connection reflected our custom of playing practical jokes on one another, a practice that helped us keep a sense of proportion in those turbulent times. Bill had asked to be included in the checkoff for the party. As secretary-treasurer I was doling out the union payroll one day, and Harry DeBoer, who had by then recovered from his injury, was collecting the party contributions. When Bill got his pay, he closed his fists around the money, shoved both hands into his pockets and told Harry: "You can have the buck if you can collect it." After wrestling Brown to the floor, rubbing some skin off his nose, and generally using him a bit roughly, DeBoer got the dollar. Bill grinned and said to Harry, "I made you earn it, you Dutch sonofabitch."

The Communist League fraction within Local 574 functioned as a single unit. Equal voice and vote was accorded to all comrades, whether they were leaders or rank-and-file members of the union. Party members in other spheres of activity were similarly organized into separate fractions in each case. These fractions were in turn part of a general branch of the party which in the given instance embraced all comrades in the city. The structure enabled those in a particular field of activity to concentrate in an organized way on their specific work. At the same time it provided a corrective for any tendency to become too narrowly engrossed in specialized activity at the expense of one's broader political education and outlook. In the case of Local 574, for example, the union problems were so pressing and so complex that comrades could easily get so one-sidedly preoccupied with them that they slighted other political and organizational matters. Being part of a general membership branch helped them to offset this danger. They were drawn into broader patterns of political thinking and into the party's multifaceted educational processes. As a result, trade-union comrades became more proficient in their own special assignments and the party was better able to help them do their job.

In addition, the party was the best medium through which trade-union comrades could keep abreast of national labor trends. Our strikes had unfolded during the fifth year of the great depression and the second year of the revival of labor. They constituted one of the three outstanding class battles of 1934, the others having been waged by the Toledo auto workers and the San Francisco longshoremen. All these strikes were led by radicals, over the opposition of conservative union officials. They tended to spill over narrow jurisdictional lines and were militantly conducted in the face of harsh police repressions. These combats not only demonstrated that the workers would and could fight for their rights—they showed that genuine rank-and-file actions could win. In all three cases the bosses were beaten and forced to recognize the union.

This series of victories gave a tremendous lift to the morale of insurgent workers throughout the country. The increasing labor momentum led to historic struggles in basic industry that resulted in the formation of the CIO and culminated in the wave of sit-down strikes that began two years later. A basic understanding on our part of this developing phenomenon was vital to the charting of Local 574's future. The mounting groundswell of labor combativity could lend us objective support in our coming battles, provided we clearly grasped the meaning of events and maintained a good sense of timing.

In more immediate terms, objective trends were already leading toward national reinforcement of our party's trade-union cadres. Parallel to the May strike in Minneapolis the American Workers Party had led the comparably militant strug-

gle of auto workers at the Electric Auto-Lite Company in
Toledo, Ohio. It had also built a substantial unemployed movement, centered in Ohio, Pennsylvania, and contiguous areas.
The AWP was centrist in character, containing both potential
revolutionaries and political opportunists. Important to us
was the presence in its ranks of militant workers who were
moving in our direction politically. A collateral consideration
was to prevent the Stalinists from knifing into the AWP while
we drew the militants over to our revolutionary program.

With this object in mind, the Communist League opened
a friendly discussion with the AWP. By December 1934 our
efforts had led to fusion of the two organizations into a new
formation called the Workers Party of the United States. Soon
after the fusion a joint national tour was made by Jim Cannon,
who had headed the Communist League of America, and A. J.
Muste, who had been the central leader of the American
Workers Party. Their arrival in Minneapolis was greeted with
great jubilation. All the comrades became doubly inspired
to go forward both in the trade-union and party-building work.

Locally our victorious strike struggle had already set the
tone, given an example, and shown the way toward further
working-class advances. In its August 24 issue the *Minneapolis
Labor Review* had declared: "Winning of this strike marks
the greatest victory in the annals of the local trade union movement. . . . It has changed Minneapolis from being known as
a scabs' paradise to being a city of hope for those who toil."

Confirmation of the declaration came swiftly. By August
27 the laundry workers, who had gone on strike after Bloody
Friday, wrested an agreement from the laundry bosses to
raise wages and improve working conditions. Their victory,
which came on the heels of Local 574's triumph, helped inspire
other workers to square off against the bosses. Strike after
strike began to take place as more and more workers joined
in the campaign to make Minneapolis a union town. In every
case help and guidance was sought from Local 574, which
had emerged as a major power in the Minnesota labor movement.

What was to happen as these new battles unfolded after 1934
proved to be no less turbulent and significant than the struggles
I have described, and no less laden with national ramifications.
Those events deserve to be related in a separate narrative.

UNITED LABOR ACTION

THE ORGANIZER
574
TWO TWENTY-FIVE SOUTH THIRD STREET
MINNEAPOLIS, MINNESOTA, WEDNESDAY, AUG. 22, 1934

SMASH THE CITIZENS ALLIANCE

VOLUME 1

NUMBER 37

VICTORY!

Settlement Goes Through!

The strike settlement adopted by the Union last night at a membership meeting is a victory for Local 574 and for the cause of trade unionism which was at stake in this strike.

The bosses, led by the Citizens Alliance, forced this strike on us. The Alliance bandits admit that they want to make this an open shop town. The beginning, they thought, would be to smash Local 574. Then they would go on to the rest of the Unions.

They have been defeated in their foul plot!

Battle - scarred and bleeding from many wounds, Local 574 rises from the struggle stronger in the confidence of the workers and more certain of its future than before.

Local 574 has not yet gotten everything for its members that it means to get. The bosses know this and we shall not let them forget it.

But what Local 574 has won is the gain of the whole union movement. All Minneapolis workers rejoice to know that the attempt to break 574 has completely fizzled and that our great union remains in the field to fight the battles of its own members and to point the road of struggle to all workers seeking the benefit of organization and a better life for themselves and their families.

The walls of Eagles hall shook last night as the members wound up their meeting with the fighting song of 574, "Solidarity Forever!"

When 574 says "Solidarity," it means union, it means stick together, fight it out, don't give in. And this is turn means 574.

This number is the veritable symbol of unionism and the unconquerable spirit of labor in Minneapolis today.

And not only in Minneapolis. Local 574's heroic struggle has become a national affair. Minneapolis has shown the country something new, and newspaper front pages everywhere carry our name.

What was new? Not the fact that a few thousand workers, miserably oppressed and exploited, rose to rebel. That happens daily. Everywhere American workers, sick of working like slaves and living like bums, are striking.

The pity is that, as a rule, they are cheated, betrayed or sold out by those they trust and

rely on. The bosses crush them, or the leaders betray them, or they get caught in the "National Run Around" of Federal mediation, and before the inexperienced workers know what has happened their strikes are broken and they go back defeated, without conditions, without a union, without anything, as a rule, but an NRA promise worth just about as much as Confederate money.

They tried all that in Minneapolis, but it was no go. That's what was new about our strike. That made the whole country sit up and take notice.

Every means of oppression was brought to bear. They shot our pickets down in cold blood. Two of them lie dead today, victims of the murdering, union-hating conspirators, martyrs to the sacred cause of labor. They flung our pickets and our leaders into a military stockade. They raided our headquarters.

But they couldn't break us.

Every dirty trick and maneuver was tried. A Farmer-Labor governor, whom so many workers trusted, turned up as a copper, throwing pickets into the stockade. They put over a "Red Scare" to see if they could catch some suckers and get the union to select a leadership to suit the bosses. Even the Federal Mediators, Father Haas and Mr. Dunnigan, to their shame, tried to go over the heads of our leaders and disrupt our ranks. Such "labor leaders" as Tobin and Smith played the rôle of Judas.

But they couldn't fool us.

Local 574 stood up and fought back. Rank and file and leaders stood united and nobody

could split us. We stuck it out and got a settlement which the whole labor movement will approve.

Thus the strike ends. But the struggle does not end.

Elections are coming. Local 574 wants to win in every house. Every worker should join the Union. Every union man should speak to his brothers on the job and see to it that 574 gets a unanimous vote. After that we shall remain vigilant and see that all conditions of the settlement are enforced in practice. Local 574 is not going to sleep at the switch.

Let's get out the vote and let's see to it that every ballot cast is marked for 574, a real union.

And a final word: Mayor Bainbridge has started to yap about driving "Communists" out of the city. We know what he means. He means framing up every worker who fights for his rights. The Citizens Alliance, sore because they had to swallow the settlement, are planning to stir their bloodhound Johannes onto some innocent individual workers and take it out of their hides.

We warn all enemies of labor: Local 574 is going to take a hand in the fight against any kind of a frame-up. Those who start this sort of business will be responsible for all the consequences.

This outlines the immediate program of Local 574:

We are going to see to it that the settlement is carried out.

We are going to win the election and build a bigger union than we ever had before.

And we are going to protect every last man of our heroic strikers against any sort of persecution.

The Organizer ceases today to be a Daily Strike Bulletin. It remains the official daily of Local 574. Until the elections have been concluded, we intend to keep it in your hands as precious weapon, a daily paper.

Numberless remarks, scores of letters give us confidence that this will be welcome news to the workers of Minneapolis.

Vote for 574 in the Elections
Make Minneapolis a Union Town

August 22, 1934, Organizer

Appendix

Allen, Ethen
Anderson, Hans
Amo, P. W.
Aboe, L.
Anderson, T.
Ardeser, F.
Abar, Wm.
Ahlquist, T.

Benzick, Bill
Bove, P.
Brown, Curly
Blais, Archie
Bolouc, Al.
Boldt, Wm. S.
Bartlett, Curly
Berman, Art.
Beal, H.
Bellanger, J.
Bensen
Bove, Rob't
Brown, Wm.
Baumgartner, Sam
Bruneau, F. D.

Croul, Elmer
Carter, Earl
Cabana, Chuck
Carle, N. E.
Costello, J.
Cipperly, Fay
Clarence, Ed.
Crichton, Minnie
Caseu, Harry
Cooper, represtative
oil co.

Devine, Joe. E.
Davis, E. B.
DeBoer, Harry
(in hospital)
Dreon, Geo.
Dobbs, Farrell
Dunne, Myles
Dunne, Grant
Dunne, Ray

Fredericks, Sam
Finklestein, Max
Frosig, Geo.

Gray, Bill

Haskell, Sam
Home, Chet.
Hallegen, Wm.

Harvey, Guy
Haynes, Harold
Hanson, John
Hall, Cliff
Holstein, Happy
Hodgekins, ERA
(Resigned)
Hoglund, Jean
Hork, Moe

Johnson, Elmer
Jossart, L. C.
Johnson, A. J.

Kneeland, Tom
Kuann
Karlen

Lundholm, E.
Levine, Ben
Lindquist, Bert
Liscombe, H. E.
(hospital)
Langeseth, Wm.
LaBeau, G. W.
Long, Bob
Lund, Bob
Lund, oil
committee rep.

Moe, Christ
Madeen, Fred
Minister, H. J.
Mathews, Clarence

Nolar, J.
Nelson, C.

Oakes, S. E.
Olson, Edith
Osborne
O'Brien, Geo.

Pfaff, Harry
Peterson, Church
Peters, Bill ERA
Resigned.
Patterson, Elmer
Pearson, W.
Postal, Kelly
Parant, Louis
Peterson, A.

Quick, C. H.
Quinn, P. F.

Rainbolt, Ray
Rogers, Johm M.
Serre, Leo

Smith, Tom
Swanson, Sam
Swenson, Melvin
Secord, Ward
Shepard, E.
Swoers, Ed.
Skoglund, Carl
Seibert, A. C.
Shedlov, Al.
Severson, Jack
Swans, Arens
Serempa, Bill
Sandell, Carl

Tutty, Don.
Taftus, R. A.
Tigue, Ray

Underwood, U. W.

Wachter, Harold
Williams, Geo.
Williams, Tom